Get Ready for Cricket

Other Titles in the Get Ready For Series:

Rugby	Barrie Corless et al
Volleyball	Rob Youngs et al
Squash	Claire Chapman et al
Soccer	Mervyn Beck et al

GET READY FOR CRICKET

A Complete Training Programme

Stuart Biddle
Peter Morris
Anne de Looy
Peter Thomas

The Crowood Press

First published in 1991 by
The Crowood Press Ltd
Gipsy Lane, Swindon
Wiltshire SN2 6DQ

British Library Cataloguing in Publication Data

Get ready for cricket : a complete training programme.
  1. Cricket
  I. Biddle, Stuart
  796.358

  ISBN 1 85223 218 8

Line-drawings by Janet Sparrow except for Figs 27, 28, 60, 62 and 63
Photographs by Allsport

Typeset by Acûté, Stroud.
Printed in Great Britain by BPCC Hazell Books, Aylesbury

Contents

The Authors

Dr STUART BIDDLE: Stuart is a lecturer in the School of Education, University of Exeter where he specialises in the psychology of physical education, and health-related fitness. He is an active consultant and author in both psychology and fitness and was previously a competitor in athletics and weightlifting, coaching the latter to international level.

Dr ANNE DE LOOY: Anne is Principal Lecturer in nutrition and dietetics at Leeds Polytechnic and is a consultant to the National Coaching Foundation on sports nutrition. She also has an active interest and involvement in cycling, rhythmic gymnastics and swimming.

PETER MORRIS: Peter is an advanced cricket coach and former minor county player, Peter is now a chartered psychologist and Principal Lecturer in sports psychology.

Dr PETER THOMAS: Peter is a general practitioner in Reading and was an Olympic oarsman in the Mexico Games of 1968. He is now the Great Britain rowing team doctor, medical director of the Reading sports injury clinic and an active consultant with the National Coaching Foundation where he was the sports medicine representative.

Introduction

Cricket is one of the traditional team games of Britain and those countries currently or previously associated with the Commonwealth. One only has to watch the extensive coverage given to the sport in the media to realise its huge following in Britain, even though it remains a mystery to sports fans in many other parts of the world.

People play sport for many different reasons, ranging from having fun, developing health and fitness, experiencing competition and making friends, to skill development. Whatever the main reason might be for playing cricket, it is quite likely that all players strive to improve or maintain their playing skills, including physical fitness. This involves preparing well for matches so that enjoyment is maximised.

These days, success in cricket (as in most sports) is usually only achieved through a well-planned and executed training pro-gramme. The purpose of this book, therefore, is to outline the fundamentals of such a training programme, although players of all levels will benefit from such preparation. Whereas most sports books, often due to the limitations of space, concentrate on the technical and tactical skills of the game, this book aims to provide a more complete picture of the training process by looking at:

(i)   skills practices
(ii)   physical fitness
(iii)   nutrition
(iv)   injury prevention
(v)   mental training

This approach is recommended as the best way of preparing yourself for the game of cricket at a time when ever-increasing demands are being made on players, and standards of skill and fitness continue to rise.

KEY

Location of stumps and batting crease	
Footmarks for initial stance (right-handed batter)	
Footmarks for the stroke	
Target for ball delivery	
Direction of ball	
Position of players	
Movement of players	
Umpire	
Cones	

1 Skills Practices

BATTING

At the start of all batting practices the batter (2) takes up an initial stance using the foot-marks which may be chalked on the floor. On the instruction 'Bat up' from the bowler (1) the bat is then lifted in line with the stumps *before* the tennis ball is thrown at the target. (No stroke should be attempted unless the delivery is accurate.) After the ball has been hit and fielded it is returned to the feeder who keeps the bowler supplied so that the practice is continuous. Players change places in rotation order after every six deliveries.

Hit to Leg off the Back Foot

(1) Played to a short-pitched ball within comfortable reach of the bat. The ball is thrown at the target to bounce waist high and the batter quickly moves back and across so that the body is square-on to the line of the ball. The bat is swung across and down with the head still and arms extended to contact the ball directly in front of the body.

(2) Wall target. The batter aims to hit the ball below a 1m line on the wall and the fielders stand on the off-side to collect the rebound.

(3) Team competition using tactics in field

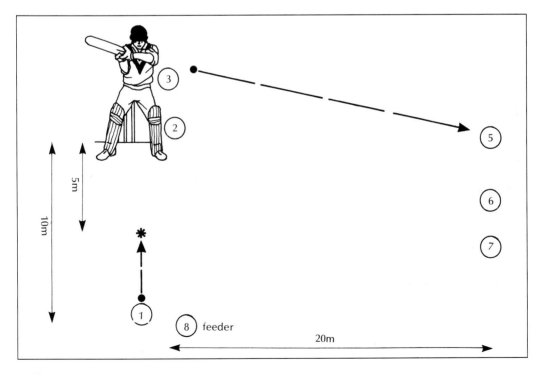

Drill 1

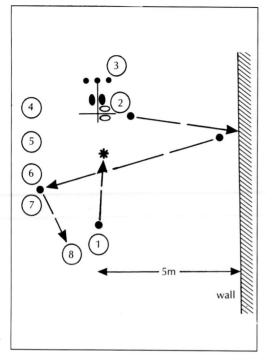

Drill 2

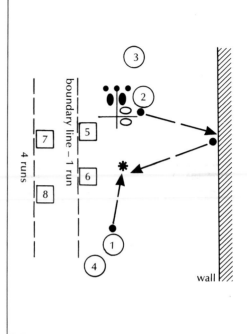

Drill 3

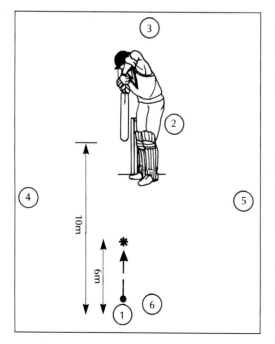

Drill 4

placing. Batters (1) and (4) versus Fielders (3) and (5).

The fielders choose where to stand, attempting to stop the ball before it crosses the boundary lines.

Back Defence

(4)   Played in defence to a short ball. The ball is thrown at the target, giving an accurate and consistent service at the start of the practice but variations in speed and trajectory may be introduced later as appropriate to the skill of the batter.

Coaching Points

(i)   The right foot is brought back parallel with the stumps to bring the head in line with the ball.

(ii)   The left elbow is lifted high with the left arm firmly in control.

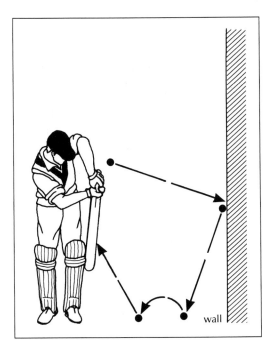

(iii)   The bat is angled down, tight into the body, and 'waits' for the ball.

(5)   Self-service. The ball is thrown by the batter at a target on the wall and the back defence stroke played at the second bounce of the rebound.

Off-Drive

(6)   Played to an over-pitched ball within comfortable driving reach on the off-side. The bowler stands close to the batter for most of the basic driving practices. On the instruction 'Bat up', the ball is dropped on to the target with the arm extended horizontally. The batter waits for the second bounce before driving the ball on the half-volley.

Drill 5

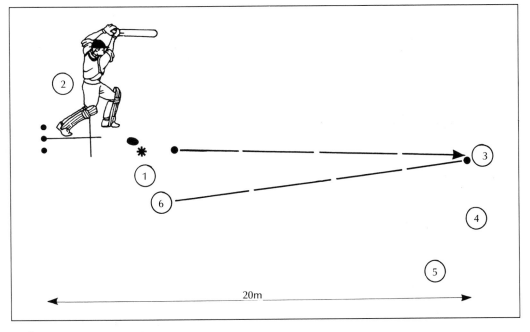

Drill 6

Coaching Points

(i)   The bat is lifted before the ball is released and the eyes are fixed on the target.

(ii)   With the head leading, the front foot is moved to the pitch of the ball.

(iii)   The bat is swung 'through' the ball with the left elbow high and the left arm controlling the stroke.

(iv)   The body remains in the sideways stance position with the head down.

Straight Drive

(7)   Played to a straight and slightly over-pitched ball within comfortable driving reach. The practice and coaching points are the same as (6), but the ball is dropped on to a target that is more in line with the off-stump.

On-Drive

(8)   Played to a slightly over-pitched ball within comfortable driving reach on the on-side. The practice and coaching points are the same as (6), but the ball is dropped on to a target that is on or just outside the line of the leg-stump.

Individual Driving Drill

(9)   The batter takes up the initial stance holding the bat in the right hand and the ball in the left. With the arm fully extended at shoulder height, the ball is dropped on to the target. The left hand is returned to grip the bat and the ball is hit on the half-volley at the second bounce.

The practice is used for the on- , off- , and straight-drive deliveries from the appropriate targets.

Moving out to Drive

(10)   Played to attack a ball that pitches too short for the normal drive.

The practice and coaching points are the same as (6), with the addition of chassé steps which the batter uses to move down the wicket. In this action the left foot moves forward, the right foot crosses behind it and the left foot goes on to the pitch of the ball. This enables the body to remain facing sideways and keeps the head at the same level throughout the stroke.

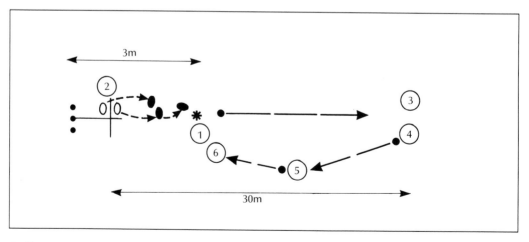

Drill 10

Lofted Drive

(11)   Played into a space to a ball within driving reach.

The practice is the same as (7), with the addition of the following coaching points.

Coaching Points

(i)   The batter moves quickly to the ball before it pitches just in front and to the off-side of the left foot.

(ii)   With the eyes fixed on the ball, the body is allowed to come up slightly as the stroke is played.

(iii)   The arms extend as the bat is swung through the ball, finishing with a high follow through.

Driving off the Front Foot

(12)   Target-aiming competition.

The practice is the same as (6). In this competition, each batter attempts to score as many target points as possible from two or more overs of six deliveries. Cones of different colours (or other markers) indicating the target areas are placed in front of the fielders. Either the cones may be repositioned, or the batter's marks adjusted to allow separate practice of the on- , off- , or straight-drive.

(13)   Run-scoring competition. Batters (1) and (3) versus Fielders (4) and (6).

The practice is the same as (6). Each team attempts to score as many target points and runs as possible from a maximum of two overs of six deliveries to each player.

The fielders, standing in front of targets, attempt to stop the ball crossing the target line. Batters may attempt to score an extra point by running round the cone and returning to the crease. In the event of a run-out, four runs are deducted from the batter's score. With both teams batting and fielding alternately, a match may be extended by adding to the number of innings.

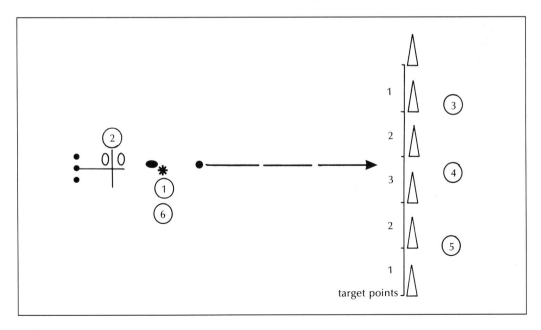

Drill 12

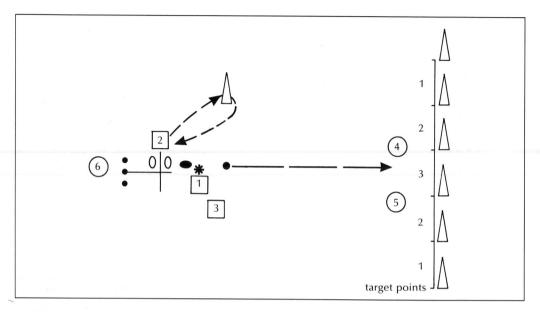

Drill 13

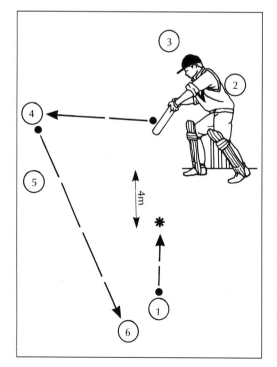

Drill 14

Square-Cut

(14) Played to a short-pitched ball wide of the off-stump.

Coaching Points

(i) The head and shoulders lead the body into the stroke with the right foot moving back and across, and the toes pointing in the direction of the intended shot.
(ii) The bat is 'thrown' out and down, arms fully extended and the weight of the body finishing on the right leg.

(15) Target-aiming competition.
   The practice is the same as (14). Each batter attempts to score as many target points as possible from a series of two or more overs. Cones of different colours are placed in front of the fielders.
   In a further variation, fielders may stand in front of the targets and attempt to stop the ball crossing the target line. To increase the press-

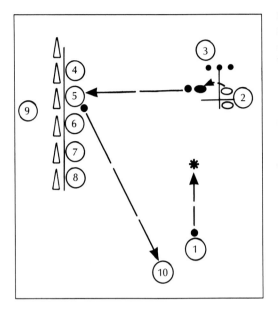

Drill 15

ure on fielders, the number in front of the line may be progressively reduced as more fielders are positioned behind the targets to retrieve the ball.

Forcing Shot off the Back Foot

(16)   Played to a short-pitched ball keeping low at knee height.

The practice is similar to (4), with the addition of the following coaching points.

Coaching Points

(i)   The ball is 'punched' away with the right hand as the left elbow is held high and the wrists firm to check the follow-through.

(ii)   The finish position shows a straight line from the top of the left elbow to the bottom of the bat, with the face 'open' and pointing in the intended direction of the ball.

Drill 16

(17)   Combined practice for the straight-, on- and off-side drive. Each player, in turn, receives a series of three overs of six deliveries (i.e. one over each for the straight-, on- and off-drive). A further series of random deliveries may be given at a later stage.

When practising the *placing* of shots, cones may be used to identify nominated target areas. The ball is thrown from a fairly low trajectory, with variations in speed being introduced later in the practice.

Forward Defence

(18)   Played in defence to a good length or slightly over-pitched ball. The ball is thrown at the target giving an accurate and consistent service at the start of the practice but variations in speed and trajectory may be introduced later as appropriate to the skill of the batter.

Coaching Points

(i)   The front foot is placed as close to the pitch of the ball as possible, with the knee slightly bent to 'close the gate' between bat and pad.
(ii)   The back leg is straight with the heel down and foot parallel with the crease to keep the sideways position.
(iii)   With the left hand in control, the handle of the bat is pushed forward to angle the face down. From this position, the ball is allowed to come on to the bat and so avoid any tendency to over-reach beyond the front foot.

(19)   Concentrated practice combining forward and backward defence. The bowler or coach throws at each target alternately, giving concentrated practice and coaching for the forward and back defensive shots. This may be followed by a series of random deliveries using both targets to provide practice in decision making about the choice of either front or back foot strokes.

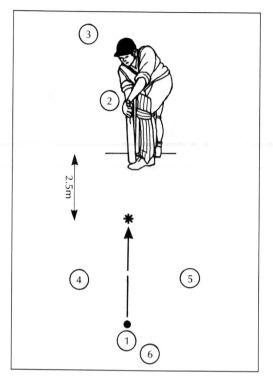

Drill 18

The Sweep

(20)   Played to a slightly over-pitched and slower ball which is on or just outside the line of the leg-stump. The ball is thrown underarm to give a low bounce and accurate service.

Coaching Points

(i)   The left foot is placed well forward into the line of the ball and the right knee bends to touch the ground.
(ii)   The bat is swung down and across, with the arms fully stretched, striking the ball on or very near the half-volley.
(iii)   The head remains still with the eyes fixed on the point of ball contact until the stroke is completed.

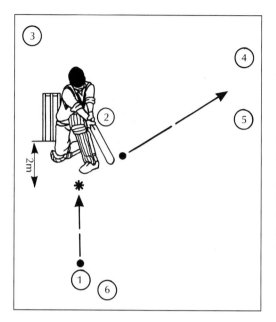

Drill 20

Hitting a Full-Toss to Leg

(21)   Played just outside the leg-stump. The ball is delivered underarm as a slow full-toss to knee height.

Coaching Points

(i)   The head is held still, looking at the point of ball contact while the left foot moves forward pointing down the pitch.
(ii)   Body weight is on front foot with the knee slightly bent.
(iii)   With the arms at full stretch, the bat is swung down and across to contact the ball directly in front of the leading leg.

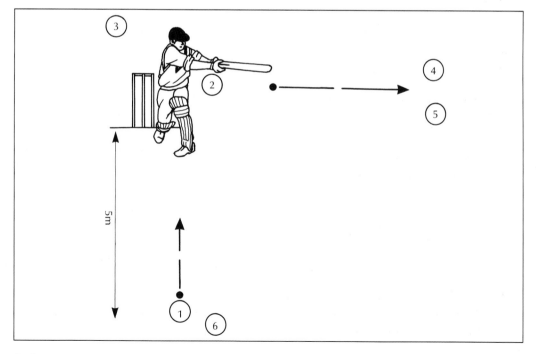

Drill 21

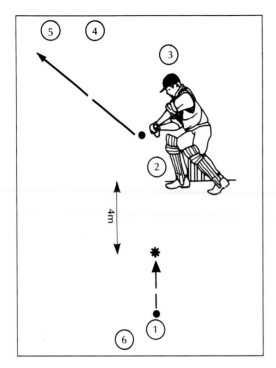

Drill 22

The Late Cut

(22)   Played to a short pitched ball well wide of the off-stump. The ball is thrown with a high, overarm action.

Coaching Points

(i)   The bat is lifted high as the right foot moves back and wide of the stumps to take the weight of the body and bring the head towards the line of the ball. An imaginary line from the left foot, extending through the right, shows the direction of the intended shot.
(ii)   The bat comes down to steer or nudge the ball into a space away from the fielders.

The Reverse Sweep

(23)   Played to an over-pitched, slower ball. This stroke should be used *only* by a skilled player who has occupied the crease for some time. The intention is to exploit a *safe* gap in

the field on the off-side, preferably with the absence of slip fielders.
   The practice is the same as (20), with the addition of the following coaching points.

Coaching Points

(i)   As the bat swings down, the left elbow is dropped and the right hand rolls over the wrists to cross the arms.
(ii)   In the change of direction the bat moves down and across with the right hand in control and the arms fully stretched.
(iii)   The ball is struck on or very near the half volley, with the emphasis on *accu- racy* rather than any great power in the shot.
(iv)   The head remains still and eyes on the point of ball contact until the stroke is completed.

The Hook

(24)   Played to a fast, short-pitched ball which has bounced at least to chest height, preferably on or just outside the leg-stump. The ball is thrown to achieve a high bounce from the target.

Coaching Points

(i)   The bat is lifted high and as early as possible before the right foot moves quickly back and across taking the head and body just outside the line of the ball (so that the ball would pass over the batter's left shoulder).
(ii)   With the bat still high, the body *pivots* through 90° over the right foot while eyes stay fixed on the ball.
(iii)   The batter should always aim to hit the ball down if there is any chance of it being caught.

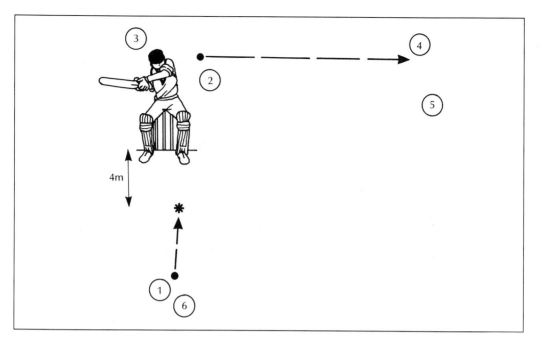

Drill 24

Backward Leg-Glance

(25)   Played to a slightly short-pitched ball which is just outside the line of the leg-stump. The ball is thrown to achieve a low bounce from the target.

Coaching Points

(i)   The right foot is moved quickly back and across to take the weight of the body. The left foot then follows close to the right to open the stance and bring the head just inside the line of the ball.

(ii)   From this position the batter waits for the ball to come on to the left hip before bringing the bat down close to the body, with the left elbow high to keep the bat upright.

(iii)   Finally, the left wrist is turned and dropped slightly to direct the ball down to the leg-side.

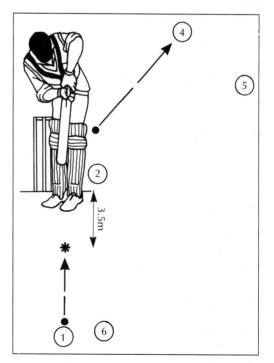

Drill 25

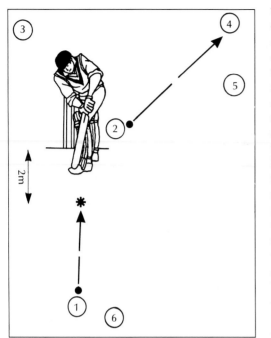

Drill 26

Forward Leg-Glance

(26)   Played to a full-length ball which is just outside the line of the leg-stump.

Coaching Points

(i)   The head leads the body into the stroke as the front leg is moved forward to land just inside the pitch of the ball.

(ii)   With the elbow high, the left hand is pushed forward to angle the bat down over the ball.

(iii)   The left wrist turns to deflect the ball off the front foot. The body is balanced in an upright position with the head over the ball.

Finding the Gaps

(27)   Before the ball is delivered the batter makes a mental note of the positions of the fielders. The service consists of three successive deliveries at each target. The batter aims to find the gaps between the fielders with appropriate ground shots off the front or back foot.

(28)   Run-scoring competition. The positions are the same as (27). Each batter attempts to score as many runs as possible from the twelve deliveries. A run is scored when the ball, travelling below waist height, crosses a line between two cones. Fielders, standing behind the cones, attempt to stop the ball before it crosses the line. All players move round one place after each twelve deliveries.

(29)   Pairs competition. The positions are the same as (27). Each pair of batters receives a total of twelve deliveries and attempts to score as many runs between the wickets as possible. The rules are:

— All deliveries must pitch within the target area.

— Fielders remain behind the cones until the ball has been hit.

— No run may be attempted to a ball that is hit above head height.

— The bowler acts as wicket-keeper.

— The bowler's feeder (7) is responsible for decisions on run-outs and on the accuracy of the service to the target.

— In the event of a run-out four runs are deducted from the total score.

The Quick Single

(30)   Pairs competition. Each pair of batters attempts to score as many single runs as possible in two overs. The pair of bowler (1) and wicket-keeper (3) change roles after the first of their two overs. The rules are:

— A wide is awarded for any ball that is judged by the umpire to have pitched outside the pitching area.

— No run may be attempted to a ball that is hit outside the boundary area of the cones.

— Four runs are deducted in the event of a run-out.

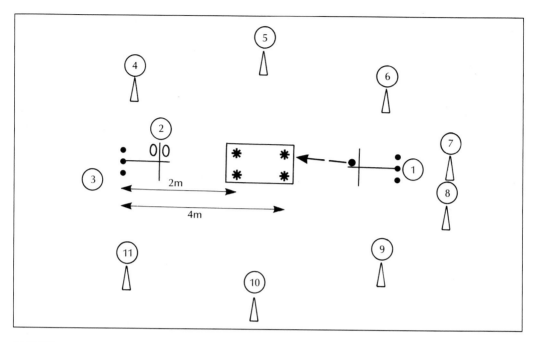

Drill 27

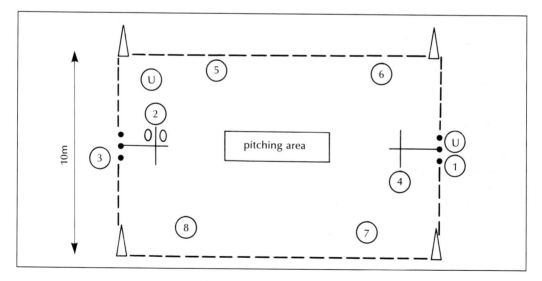

Drill 30

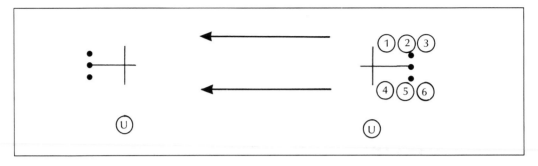

Drill 31

Running Between the Wickets

(31) One against one and a team competition. When the umpire calls 'Run', the first players in each team race each other to the opposite popping crease. The winner is the first player to ground the bat beyond the crease. The next two players move up to the starting position with their bats in contact with the ground behind the crease. The winning team is the one who records the most number of individual winners. The race is repeated with the players running in the opposite direction (maximum four races).

(32) Team relay. When the umpire calls 'Run', the first player in each team (1) and (5) race to the opposite popping crease. The next player starts the return run as soon as the bat of the incoming player has crossed the line of the crease. The winning team is the first to complete the relay.

(33) Warm-up team relay. Each player must ground the bat behind the line at both ends. When the teams consist of five or more players, the race may be continuous with up to three runs for each player.

(34) Deciding when to run; pairs competition. The players are grouped in pairs, with each pair changing position every two overs, i.e: (1) and (2)→(3) and (4)→(5) and (6), etc. Play begins when one of the pair of batters throws the ball (underarm) to any point within the boundary area. The batters may start to run as soon as the ball leaves the hand. (Batters are encouraged to *call* for runs, and may decide not to run on every ball.)

The objective of the batters is to score as many runs as possible within their two overs. In the event of a run-out or catch the batting pair deduct four runs from their score.

WICKET-KEEPING

Coaching Points

Normally, gloves should be worn and a hard ball used in all wicket-keeping practices outdoors. A tennis ball should be used for wall-practices and whenever gloves are not available.

(i) Wicket-keeping begins with the initial stance (or ready position). The body is well-balanced (weight on the balls of the feet) in a comfortable crouch position, with the knees pointing down the wicket.

(ii) Standing up to the wicket:
— The left foot is behind the off- stump. The head is close to the stump in a line with the leg-stump at the bowler's end.
— the hands are close together between the knees and hips and on the line of the ball.
— Fingers point down and the elbows are tucked in close to the body to make the catching area as large and compact as possible.

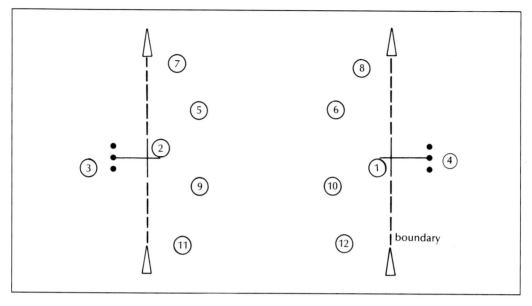

Drill 34

(iii)   To receive a ball which is just outside the off-stump:
— The hands and hips move to the line and wait for the ball. For balance and safety, the head and shoulders are 'left behind' inside the line of the ball.
— The body remains in the crouched position, with the head and knees staying the same distance apart.
— the body rises with the ball to a straight leg position and the hands give slightly to meet the impact. After every catch the ball is quickly and automatically taken to the stumps. The ball is caught at the side of the body, not in front of the chest.

(iv)   To receive a ball which is wider on the off-side:
— The left foot stays inside the semi-circle and the right foot moves in a straight line parallel with the stumps.
— The ball is caught with the hands in front of the right hip with the fingers pointing to the side.
— The elbows remain tucked into the body

with the head just inside the line of the ball.

(v)   To receive a ball on the leg-side:
— The right foot stays and the left foot moves to take the left hip and the weight of the body into the line of the ball.

(vi)   To receive a ball at a distance away from the stumps:
— It is probably quicker to turn and run to the line of the ball (watching it closely all the time) than to side-step.

(35)   Standing-up. Both players take up the initial crouch position with the head close-to and in line with the off-stump at the opposite end. A tennis ball is thrown to a point just outside and above the off-stump. Players practice the technique of moving from the crouch to take the ball at hip height.

A variation is to throw the ball (overarm) to bounce to hip height just outside the off-stump. This provides practice in straightening the legs and body as the ball lifts from the pitch.

23

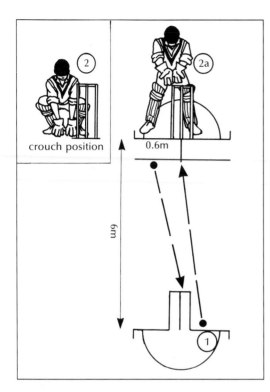

Drill 35

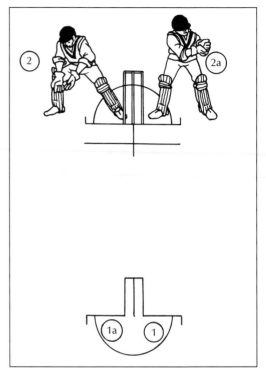

Drill 36

(36) Moving sideways. Both players take up the crouch position inside the semi-circle which is marked on the ground. A tennis ball is thrown to a point wide of the stump at a catchable height (i.e. between the knee and the shoulder). Deliveries are varied between the off- and leg-side and include slower balls which are aimed to land about two or three metres away from the stump. Players practice the footwork and other points of technique for receiving the ball away from the stump.

(37) Behind the batter. The ball is thrown to any point within the pitching area, with variation appropriate to the skill of the wicket-keeper. The batter moves to play the ball but intentionally misses each delivery. This is intended to give the wicket-keeper practice under more realistic conditions. With each stop, the wicket-keeper quickly takes the ball to the stumps in one continuous movement.

(38) Catching. The ball is thrown to the target as a short-pitched delivery wide of the off-stump. The batter uses a cricket stump to play a square-cut, creating realistic catching chances for the wicket-keeper.

(39) Field catching. The ball is rolled by the feeder (1) to any one of the fielders and quickly returned over the stumps to the wicket-keeper. Close fielders use an underarm return.

(40) Run-outs. The bowler rolls or throws the ball to any one of the fielders who returns it to the wicket-keeper in an attempt to run-out the incoming batter. The batter starts to run as soon as the ball leaves the bowler's hand. The position of the fielders may be adjusted to give both the wicket-keeper and batters an equal chance of success.

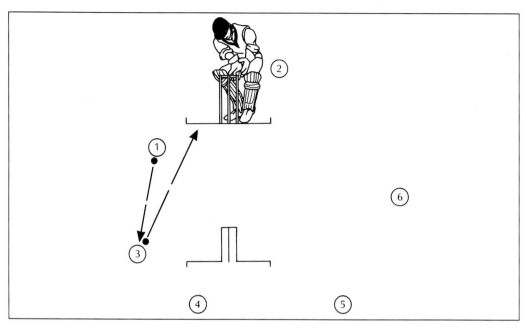

Drill 39

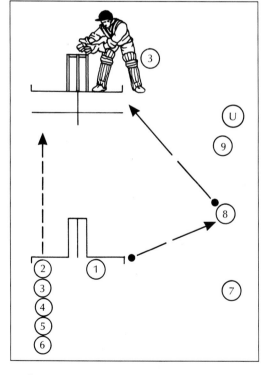

Drill 40

Practice is continuous as the next batter moves up to the popping crease when the ball is returned by the wicket-keeper to the bowler. The practice may be repeated when the batters assemble at the opposite end and the bowler and wicket-keeper change ends.

(41) Fielding. The bowler rolls the ball into a fielding area near the wicket-keeper who is standing with one foot on a marker behind the stumps. As soon as the ball leaves the bowler's hand the first batter (4) starts to run and the wicket-keeper attempts to run the batter out by returning the ball to a second wicket-keeper (2) at the bowler's end. The wicket-keeper discards a glove before collecting and throwing the ball at the stumps.

The bowler acts as umpire in any run-out decisions. Practice is repeated with batters (5) and (6), and may be continued with the bowler and wicket-keeper changing ends. The bowler may roll the ball in any direction and at an appropriate speed to give the wicket-keeper varied practice and a fair chance of running the batter out.

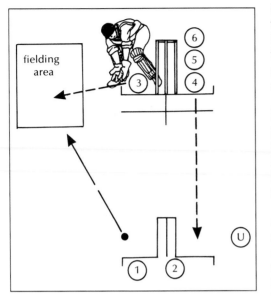

Drill 41

(42) Stumping. The bowler throws the ball to the pitching area at a speed or with spin that is intended to beat the bat. The batter plays forward defence strokes to every delivery and periodically and intentionally misses the ball and lifts or drags the back foot over the crease.

The practice may include stumpings on the leg-side for deliveries to the alternative pitching area.

(43) High catching. The batter (2) hits the ball at varying heights to any point within the hitting area. The wicket-keeper (3) tries to catch the ball and then returns it to the feeder (1).

The shots are made to represent a mis-hook on the leg-side or a top-edge to short third man position.

(44) Saving byes. The ball is thrown at speed to bounce at varying heights from the off- or leg-side pitching areas whilst the wicket-keeper, standing back, attempts to stop it. Fielders (3) and (4) retrieve any byes and return the ball to the feeder (5).

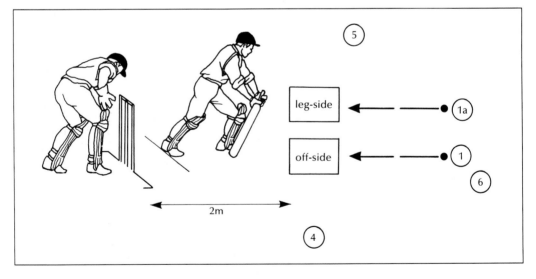

Drill 42

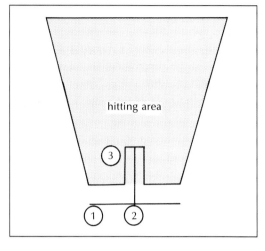

Drill 43

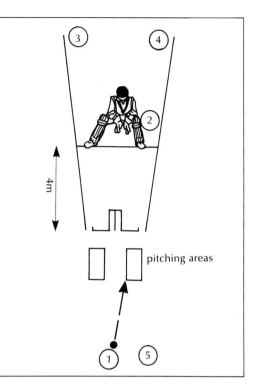

Drill 44

The practice may be run as a competition, with one point scored for each ball stopped, and the feeder acting as umpire in decisions on fair stops and deliveries outside the target areas.

(45) Diving catches. The ball is thrown underarm at a catching height above the mats on either side of the stumps. The direction, height and speed of each delivery are varied. The wicket-keeper takes up the initial stance position before each delivery and attempts to achieve as many catches as possible. Fielders are used to return the ball to the bowler or feeder.

The practice may be run as a competition with each player scoring as many catches as possible from a set number of deliveries.

(46) Wall practice. The wicket-keeper takes up the initial stance position before bouncing or throwing the ball underarm and catching the rebound from the wall.

Practice begins with a series of catches from the 4m mark before moving closer to the wall where quicker reactions are needed.

(47) Wall practice — variation 1. The wicket-keeper takes up the initial stance facing the wall in the semi-circle behind the stumps and

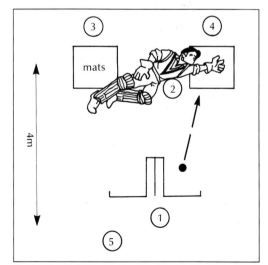

Drill 45

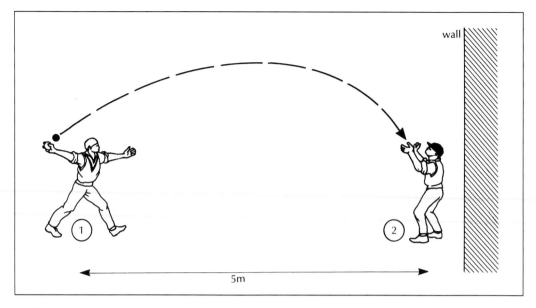

Drill 50

attempts to catch the ball as it rebounds from the wall. The ball is thrown underarm by the bowler who stands just behind the wicket-keeper. As the wicket-keeper becomes more proficient, the difficulty may be increased by projecting the ball at different speeds and angles.

(48)   Wall practice — variation 2. The ball is thrown underarm at the wall for the batter to half-volley a straight-drive using a cricket stump as a bat. The wicket-keeper attempts to catch any mis-hit, to stump the batter, or field the ball, as appropriate. The fielder (4) acts also as a feeder to return each ball for the bowler to provide a continuous service.

(49)   Pressure practices. The ball is thrown in sets of six continuous deliveries for the practice of a wide range of wicket-keeping skills. Fielder (3) may be used to stop the ball and return it to the feeder if a suitable wall is not available.

The practice provides an opportunity for a coach, acting as the bowler, to introduce or develop points of technique and concentrate on any particular weaknesses (e.g. leg-side stumping, high and low catching).

A variation, for more skilled players, is to throw the ball into a slip cradle in front of the stumps, or on to an area of rough ground, to increase the difficulty and reduce the predictability of each delivery.

BOWLING

(50)   The windmill action. The objectives are to develop the sideways stance and a high, straight-arm delivery.

The bowler stands sideways, feet apart. The arm is extended parallel with the ground at shoulder height, holding the ball in the fingers. The ball is lobbed to a partner or at a target marked on a wall 2m from the ground.

Coaching Points

(i)   Look over the left shoulder to the target.
(ii)   With the arms out straight, the body rocks or levers over the left side.
(iii)   Release the ball at the highest point above the left shoulder (i.e. at 12 o'clock high).

(51)   The coil position. The objectives are the same as (50), with the addition of directional accuracy.

Coaching Points

(i)   Keep the sideways stance with the body weight on the rear leg.
(ii) Stretch the left arm up high and look at the stumps from behind the elbow.
(iii) Coil the right arm across the chest.
(iv) Pull the left arm down the line of the target.
(v)   Lever the body, still in the sideways positions, over the left side.
(vi) Uncoil the right arm and release the ball at the highest point above the left shoulder.
(vii) Follow through with the right hand past the left hip.

(52) The bound. The objective is to change the forward run-up to the sideways stance.

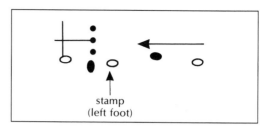

Drill 52

Coaching Points

(i)   Walk slowly forward and stamp left foot into the ground as the body begins to turn sideways.
(ii) Continue the sideways turn with a short, high cross-over step with the right foot. (The knee is lifted high and close to the body).
(iii) The left leg now makes a long stride to complete the 90° sideways turn and take the body into the coil position.
(iv) Repeat the practice, moving up to the popping crease. Chalk marks may be used to show the feet positions.

(53) The short run-up. The objective is to develop body momentum in the approach.

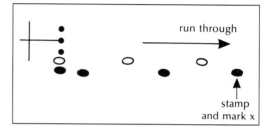

Drill 53 (i)

Coaching Points

(i)   From a standing position at the side of the stumps, mark the distance of a comfortable five pace run-up, straight back from the stumps.
(ii) Start the run-up with the right foot, taking short strides and gradually increasing speed.
(iii) Stand with both feet level with the mark and practise the run-up to the stumps. Start off with the right foot so that the left hits the ground in the correct position for the bound.

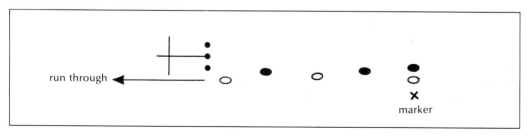

Drill 53 (ii)

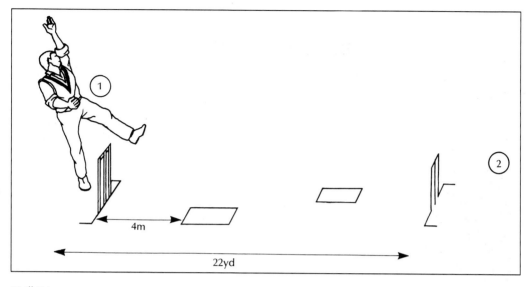

Drill 54

(54) The basic bowling action. The objectives are to develop a consistent and rhythmic bowling action, and to improve length and direction.

Practise bowling to a partner or target on a wall (Cones or chairs may be used in place of stumps). The bowler moves to the wicket-keeping position to receive the return delivery from a partner. Remember that the run-up should be marked and checked at the start of the practice. When the direction (line) of the bowling is consistent and accurate, the size of the target may be reduced (e.g. to one off-stump). Accuracy in the length of delivery may be checked by a mark on the ground (approximately 4m from the off-stump) but the stump, and not the mark, remains the bowler's target.

The classic bowling action of Terry Alderman (Australia).

(55) Spinning the ball clockwise. The objective is to spin the ball using the wrist and fingers.

The bowler stands at approximately 45° to a partner, or a target on the wall, with the arm held high above the head. The elbow is straight and the hand holding the ball points to the target. The arm is pulled down towards the target and the wrist and fingers turn sharply to release the ball at head height. The movement of the wrist is like turning the handle to open a door.

The ball is held loosely between the thumb and the first two fingers. The index finger, pulling along the seam, gives the most spin to the ball. The bowling arm remains as straight as possible throughout the delivery. A rotation of the shoulders and body to face the target may be added to the movement as the practice is continued.

(56) Off-spin bowling. The objective is to develop a fluent and effective action for the off-spin delivery.

An area is marked to indicate the pitch of the ball on a good length and just outside the

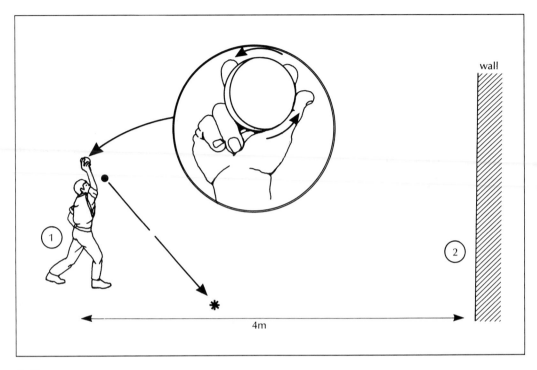

Drill 55

line of the off-stump. Each bowler measures and marks the run-up and aims to hit the off-stump with the ball pitching on the marked area.

Coaching Points

(i)   Close the basic stance slightly by placing the left foot more towards the leg-side.
(ii)   The ball is released high above the right shoulder as the body pivots and the arm pulls against the left side of the body.
(iii)   Bring the right knee across high and close to the body to assist the pivot action.

(57)   Spinning the ball anti-clockwise. The objective is to spin the ball using the wrist and fingers.

The ball is loosely gripped with the fingers and thumb fairly evenly spaced around the seam. In a kneeling position the player holds the ball on the ground and spins it anti-clockwise on its vertical axis.

Progression to short-arm spinning is made from a sideways stance, the right arm held at shoulder height with the elbow and the wrist almost fully bent. The elbow remains bent as the forearm is brought over and the wrist rotates to spin the ball. The arm may be straightened and the distance between the players extended as the practice continues.

(58)   Leg-spin bowling. The objective is to develop a consistent and effective action for the leg-spin delivery.

An area is marked to indicate the correct pitch of the ball on a good length in line with the leg- and middle-stump. The bowler aims to hit the off-stump with a ball that pitches in line with the leg- or middle-stump.

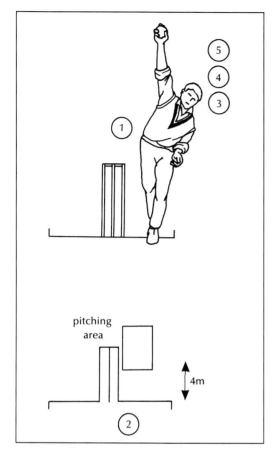

Drill 56

Coaching Points

(i)   The basic bowling action is used with the sideways stance through the coil position as in (54).

(ii)   The left shoulder is dropped slightly and the wrist fully bent as the ball is flipped and spun off the third finger.

(iii)   The rotation of the wrist and fingers is kept in the sideways position with the action and follow through of the arm in line with the off-stump.

The top-spin can be developed from this action, with the addition of coaching points:

Coaching Points

(i)   The leg-spin action is used with the rotation of the wrist and fingers in line with the middle-stump.

(ii)   The beginner might find it easier to bowl the top-spinner by turning the wrist so that more of the back of the hand is pointed towards the batter.

(iii)   The ball is aimed to pitch in the line of the middle-stump.

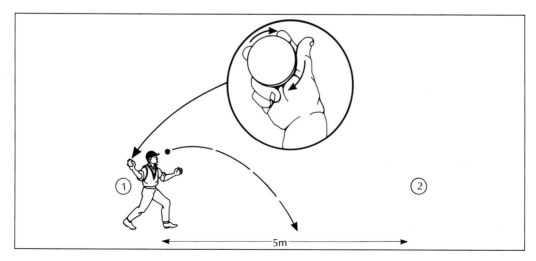

Drill 57

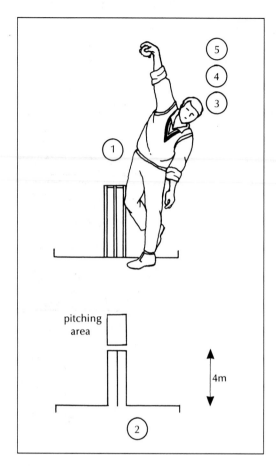

Drill 58

The googly, also, can be developed, with the addition of the following coaching points:

Coaching Points

(i)   The leg-spin action is used but the back of the wrist is pointed towards the batsman.
(ii)   The rotation of the wrist begins earlier, before the ball is released, and both the third and little fingers are used to spin the ball.
(iii)   The action may be assisted by placing the left foot slightly to the left side to achieve a more open stance, and by dropping the left shoulder to enable the back of the hand to

lead the palm in a line which is just outside the leg-stump.
(iv)   The bowler aims to pitch the ball in line with the middle-stump.

(59)   Left-arm spin bowling. The objectives are to pitch the ball consistently on or just outside the off-stump, and to achieve variations in flight and pace.

Coaching Points

For the leg-break: (left arm)
(i)   The grip and basic bowling action is similar to that of the right-arm off-spin bowler.
(ii)   The delivery is usually made close to and around the wicket to the right-hand batter.
(iii)   Variations may be achieved by using the full width of the crease.
(iv)   To a left-hand batter the delivery is usually made from over the wicket (unless achieving a considerable spin on the ball).
(v)   The ball is aimed well up to the batter on the line of the middle-stump.
(vi)   Accuracy of line is more important than spin.

Coaching Points

For the off-break (or Chinaman):
(i)   To the right-hand batter, the grip and basic bowling action is similar to that of the right-arm leg-spin bowler. The delivery is aimed at the off-stump (with a strong field placing on the leg-side and a slip fielder for the googly).

India's Kapil Dev. A classic fast bowling action that relies on good technique and a well-maintained body.

shiny surface

Drill 60

(60) In-swing bowling. The objective is to make the ball swing in to the stumps in the last part of its flight. It is important that the seam remains vertical throughout the flight. It may be useful to practise with a ball that has two sides of different colours or a chalked seam that can be seen during the flight.

Coaching Points

(i) Open the basic bowling action slightly by placing the front foot towards the off-side.
(ii) Look at the stumps from 'inside' the leading arm.
(iii) Release the ball at the highest point above the head and follow through in line with the stumps down towards the right hip.
(iv) Hold the ball with the first two fingers close together on top of the seam and the thumb underneath.
(v) Point the seam towards the fine-leg position with the shiny side of the ball facing the batter.

(61) Out-swing bowling. The objective is to make the ball swing away from the stumps in the last part of its flight.

Coaching Points

(i) Hold the ball with the first two fingers either side of the seam and the inside of the thumb on the bottom of the seam.
(ii) Keep the seam vertical and pointing to the first slip position with the shiny side of the ball facing the batter.
(iii) Close the basic bowling action slightly by placing the front foot towards the on-side.
(iv) The body pivots as the arm is brought across the chest and down past the left hip.
(v) Aim the ball to pitch in line with the stumps. When the seam hits the ground the deviation may be increased.

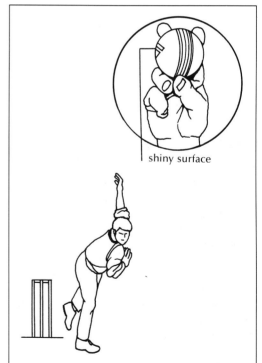

shiny surface

Drill 62

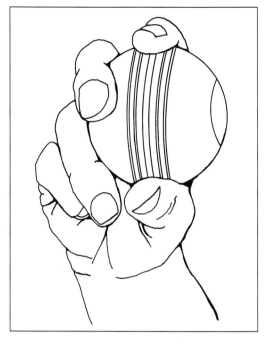

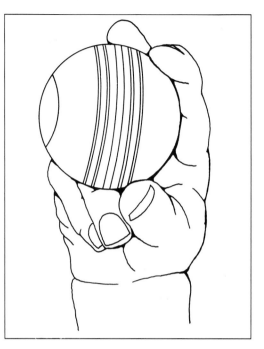

Drill 62   *Drill 63*

(62)   Medium-pace bowling — the off-cutter. The objective is to move the ball off the pitch in to the stumps at a medium or fast pace.

Coaching Points

(i)   Hold the ball with the first two fingers fairly close together. The index finger is placed along the top of the seam and the thumb underneath.

(ii)   The seam is vertical and points towards the stumps.

(iii)   The ball is 'cut' by pulling the index finger and wrist down in a fast, clockwise movement.

(iv)   The basic bowling action is used for the off-cutter which is a useful delivery for the out-swing bowler.

(63)   Medium-pace bowling – the leg-cutter. The objective is to move the ball off the pitch and away from the bat towards or just outside the off-stump.

Coaching Points

(i)   Hold the ball with the first two fingers fairly close together. The second finger is placed along the top of the seam and the thumb underneath.

(ii)   The ball is 'cut' by pulling the second finger down in a fast, anti-clockwise movement.

(iii)   The basic bowling action is used for the leg-cutter which is a useful delivery for the in-swing bowler.

(64)   Fast bowling. The objectives are:
—   To make the batter play at every delivery.
—   To keep the ball well-up to the bat, although some variation in length may unsettle the batter.

Drill 64

— To pitch the ball on the seam in an attempt to make it deviate from the line of flight.
— To vary the pace slightly and occasionally in an attempt to deceive the batter.

Coaching Points

(i)   It is important for a fast bowler to warm-up and loosen-up very thoroughly before bowling.

(ii)   The length of the run-up should be just sufficient to achieve an effectively fast and controlled body momentum. This enables the weight of the body to be transferred on to the back leg in the bound movement before delivery.

(iii)   The run-up involves a gradual acceleration and requires a lot of practice to achieve consistency and avoid the no-ball.

(iv)   The delivery is usually bowled from over the wicket and close to the stumps with a full swing of the bowling arm.

(v)   The speed of the ball gives the batter less time to decide and play the stroke. Slight variations of speed and length will add to this indecision. The length may force the batter to play a non-preferred stroke (i.e. off the front or back foot). To achieve this the fast bowler should know before-hand what type of stroke the batter prefers to play.

(vi)   Variations in the length of the ball usually range from a yorker, which pitches at the batter's feet, to a short ball which bounces to chest height. The condition of the ball and the bounce of the pitch will determine the correct length of the short-pitched delivery. The fast bowler should be encouraged to watch and work out these decisions beforehand.

(vii)   Fast bowling requires a high level of fitness, suppleness and strength (particularly in the legs and back). Physical preparation is an important part of practice.

FIELDING

(65)   Throwing. Alternate throwing and catching with a partner, aiming at a target area which is the width of the body, below the shoulders and above the waist.

This practice can progress to a competition, where the winner is the first player to score ten target hits. A single player may use the same practice over a distance of 5m, aiming at a target of the same size marked on a wall.

Coaching Points

(i)   Sideways stance with feet wide apart and weight on the back leg.
(ii)   The body is slightly bent at the hips, eyes fixed on the target.
(iii)   The right arm is stretched back behind the right shoulder and the left arm points at the target.
(iv)   The right arm is brought across at shoulder height in a whip-like action.

(66)   Stopping — the Long Barrier. The ball is rolled towards the partner who stops and returns it with a fast and accurate overarm throw.

In competition, both players aim to roll the ball below knee height between the opponent's skittles. The winner is the first player to score ten goals. Additional players (3) and (4) may act as feeders and take their turn in the competition.

Coaching Points

(i)   The long barrier is used when the ball is travelling on an unpredictable path (e.g. over uneven ground).
(ii)   The body pivots, allowing the knee to drop to the ground in front of the opposite foot. The leg and foot form the long barrier.
(iii)   The ball is stopped with both hands together in front of the leg.
(iv)   A fast and accurate return is aimed at the player's chest.

(67)   Stopping — the Short Barrier. The fielder (2) moves quickly towards the approaching ball, stops and returns it to the feeder (1). Practice may include both overarm and underarm returns.

In competition, any number of players, working in pairs, may take part. The ball may not be stopped before it has crossed the 15m line. The fielder (2) must stand behind the starting line before the ball is released. The

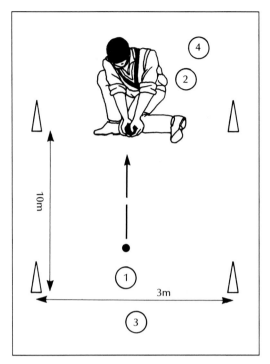

Drill 66

winning pair is the first to manage six complete returns.

Coaching Points

(i)   The short barrier is used when the ball is travelling on a fairly predictable path some distance away from the wicket.
(ii)   The fielder moves quickly to intercept.
(iii)   The ball is stopped with both hands in front of the leading right foot which is placed across the line of the ball.
(iv)   The body is bent low to the ground before reaching the ball.
(v)   When the ball is travelling slow or has stopped, the pick-up is made close to the outside of the left foot.
(vi)   A further pace is taken with the left foot around which the body pivots into the sideways throwing position.

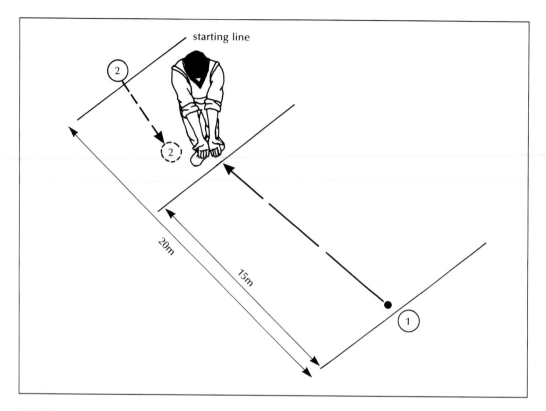

starting line

20m

15m

1

2

2

Drill 67

(68)   Retrieving. The fielder (2) runs to retrieve the ball and returns it with an overarm throw to the feeder (1). The ball is rolled at varying speeds but the fielder remains behind the starting line until it is released.

Competition is one pair against another. The ball may not be stopped before it has crossed the 10m line. Players change places after each set of six runs. The winning pair is the first to complete four sets of runs.

Coaching Points

(i)   When the ball is travelling fast, the pick-up is made close to the outside of the right foot, with the body bent low to the ground.
(ii)   Two further steps are taken to check forward movement as the body is turned through 180° to the sideways position for the overarm throw back to the feeder.

(69)   Intercepting close to the wicket. The ball is rolled in turn to each of the fielders (2) to (5). Each of them runs in and throws under-arm back to the feeder/wicket-keeper (1).
(70)   Boundary fielding. The ball is hit or thrown by the batter towards the boundary. The first fielder runs to intercept, returns the ball to the wicket-keeper and continues on to the back of the team. Fielders wait behind the line of the skittles until the ball is hit before moving to intercept.

Fielders may be divided into two teams, standing in separate lines and intercepting alternate shots. The winning team is the one that concedes the least number of boundaries.

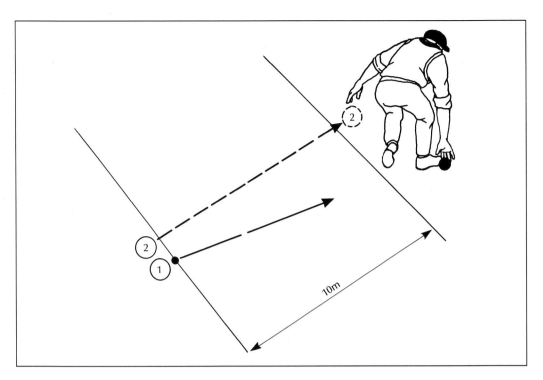

Drill 68

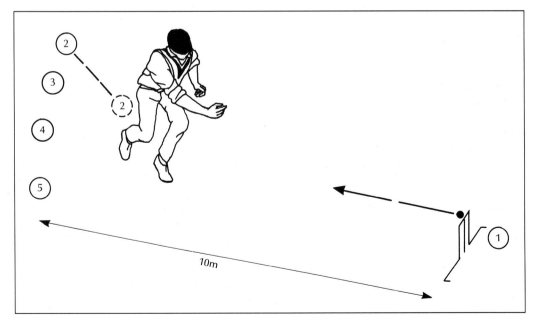

Drill 69

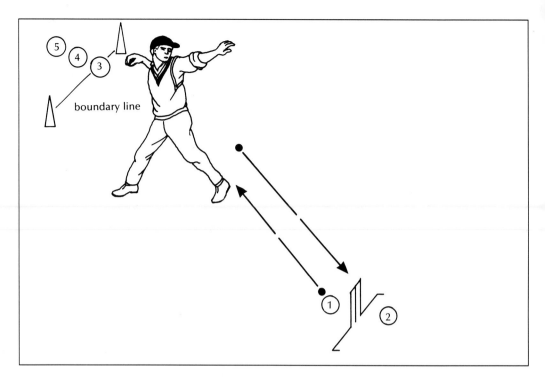

boundary line

Drill 70

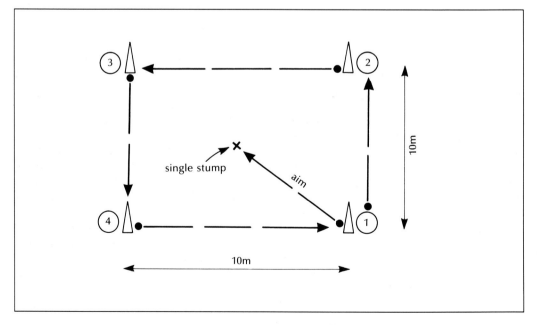

single stump

aim

10m

10m

Drill 71

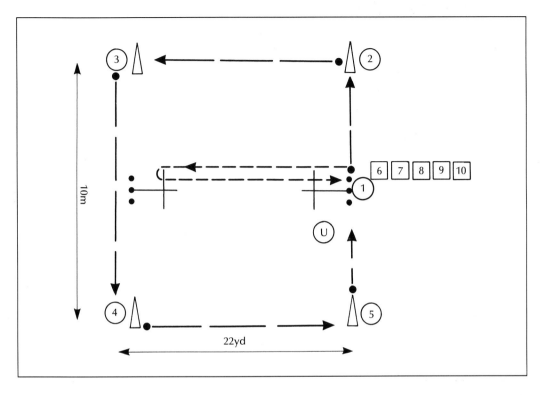

Drill 72

(71) Fielding target race. The objective is to hit the target (a single stump) as many times as possible within a given time period.

The ball is quickly passed to each player on the four corners of the square. When the ball returns to the starting point, the player who started the passing sequence has the chance of scoring a point by aiming an underarm throw at the target. The player nearest to the ball immediately retrieves it and restarts the passing sequence. The race may be run against a set time or in competition with other groups of players.

(72) Team passing to run-outs. The objective is for each player in the batting team to score a return run before being run-out.

The ball is rolled by the wicket-keeper (1) to the first fielder (2) and then passed to each corner of the square and back to the wicket-keeper. This is repeated for each batter.

Each player attempts to complete a run before the ball is returned to the stumps.

(73) Intercepting — variation 1. Team competition. The ball is rolled past the 10m line to each of the fielders (2) to (6) in turn. They attempt to run-out the incoming player in the batting team. The winning team is one that successfully completes the most number of runs from the five attempts that are given to each team. The rules are:

— The ball may not be intercepted by the fielder until it has crossed the 10m line.

— The batter may not start to run before the ball is released by the feeder/wicket-keeper.

43

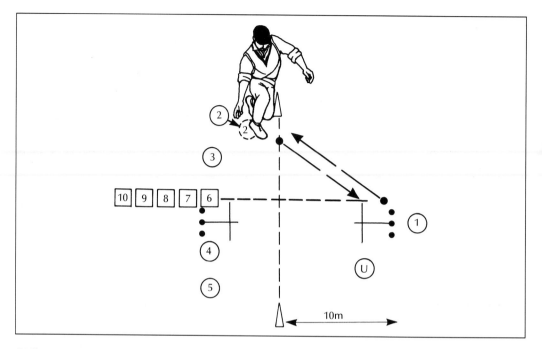

Drill 73

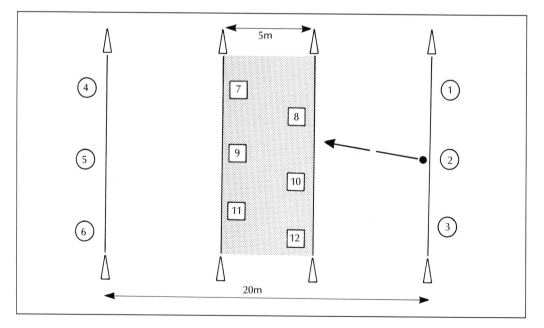

Drill 74

Coaching Points

The running underarm throw.
(i)   The player moves in quickly with the body low, head down and eyes on the ball.
(ii)   The ball is picked-up alongside the right foot and released in one fast movement as the arm follows through to the target.

(74)   Intercepting — variation 2. Three-court stopping. The middle team attempts to stop the ball from passing through its territory. The rules are:
—   The ball must be rolled below knee height from behind the sidelines. Existing floor markings may be used in preference to skittles to indicate the three court boundaries.
—   When a larger number of players take part, the middle team may stand in two separate lines towards the front edge of their court, facing their nearest opponents.
        In this case more than one tennis ball may be in play at the same time.
—   The teams change positions after a set period of time (e.g. 60 seconds).
—   A competition may be introduced in which the winning team is the one that manages to score the most number of passes with-in the allotted playing time.

(75)   Aiming relay. At the starting signal the first players in each team run forward, place the ball on a line between the centre skittles and continue on to the back of the team. When the player has crossed the line the next runs to pick up, throw (underarm) to the opposite player and continue to the back of the team. The sequence of alternative placing and throwing continues until all players have completed each task twice.

(76)   Low catching. Catching between two players using quick, underarm throws which can be caught without moving the feet.

    Competition utilises skittles or wall markings to indicate the catching area. The winner is the first player to make ten catches.

Coaching Points

(i)   Feet are comfortably apart with the bodyweight evenly distributed on the balls of the feet.
(ii)   Knees and hips are bent low, the body stays down and the head remains still.
(iii)   The hands are together and pointing down with the palms wide open.
(iv)   The eyes are fixed on the ball.

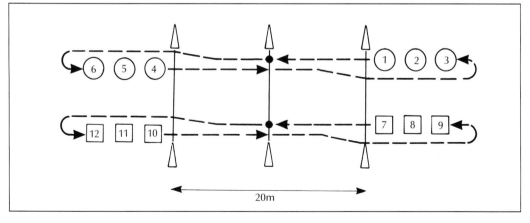

Drill 75

45

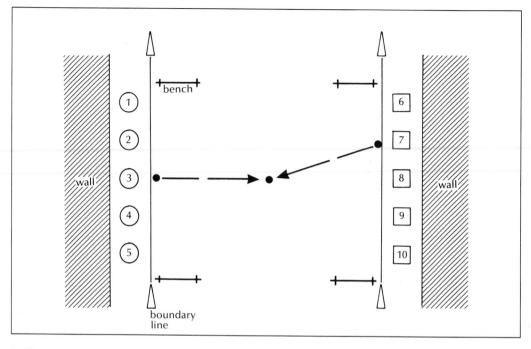

Drill 77

(77) Aiming — crossfire team game. The objective is to hit the ball across the opponents' boundary line.

Either one or several tennis balls may be used, depending on the number of players. An end wall or benches are useful in keeping the target ball within the throwing area. Players are required to remain behind the boundary line when fielding and throwing the ball.

(78) Backing-up. Three fielders are positioned at the marked corners of a square and a single cricket stump is placed in the middle. The objective is for each player to score as many direct hits on the stump as possible.

After the first throw, player (1) quickly moves in a clockwise direction to the next corner of the square. At the same time player (2) moves to replace player (1). The first throw is fielded by player (3) who then throws at the stump and moves to replace player (2). The sequence is continued with each player having the same

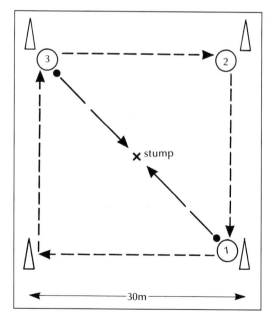

Drill 78

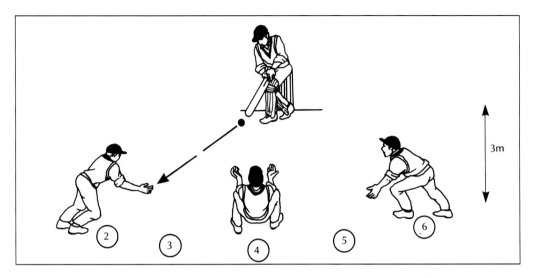

Drill 79

number of practices in aiming and backing-up.

Variations can be gradually introduced, as follows:

— The distances of the sides of the square may be reduced to increase pressure on the fielders.

— Over short distances (i.e. less than 10m), players may practise moving in for a fast underarm throw.

— Additional players may be included at different points that are marked by cones. With several players taking part, a circle is formed with the target in the centre.

(79)   Close catching. The ball is hit with a bat from a low position to any one of the close fielders (2) to (6).

Competition progresses so that each fielder, in turn, receives one set of six deliveries (all within catching reach without moving the feet). The winner is the player who completes the most catches.

(80)   Slip-catching. The ball is thrown as a medium-fast full-toss, to pass just outside the off-stump at chest height. From here it is deflected off the face of the bat which is angled towards the slip fielders. Practice is continuous as each attempted catch is returned to the feeder.

Coaching Point

It is important for each fielder to expect to receive every delivery and to watch the ball from the moment it leaves the bowler's hand.

(81)   Surprise catching. The objective is to catch the ball before it lands on the mat in the centre of the circle.

The centre player (7) rolls the ball to any person in the circle and immediately changes places with another player who attempts to catch the ball when it is lobbed back into the centre. It is preferable to use a thick mat to mark the centre of the circle and provide a soft landing for the diving catch.

(82)   Slip cradle catching. The ball is thrown overarm into the slip cradle for fast, continuous catching on both sides.

In team competition, the winners are the pair who complete the most catches from a set number of throws. Progressive difficulty can be increased by placing a screen (e.g. a sight-

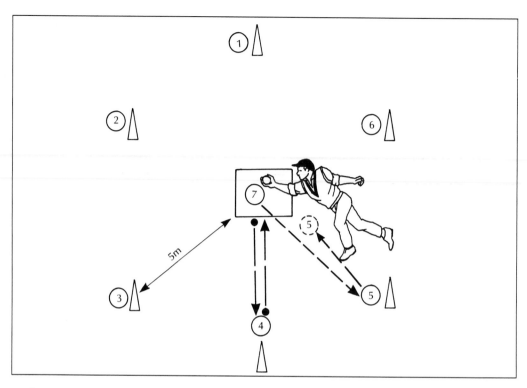

Drill 81

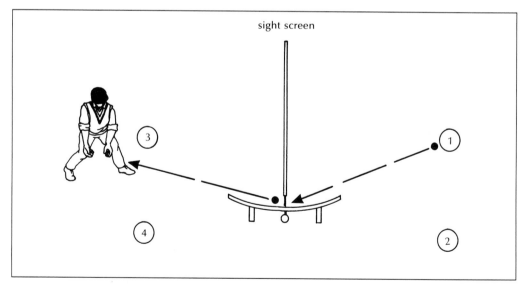

Drill 82

screen) above the middle of the cradle to obscure the view of the player throwing the ball.

(83) Wall catching. The fielder (2) stands in the low catching position and attempts to catch the ball when it rebounds from the wall. The feeder (1) may vary the speed, trajectory and angle of delivery to increase the difficulty of the catch.

This practice can progress to corner catching. A corner of the room may be used, together with a variation of direct and bounced deliveries using two walls to increase the difficulty.

(84) Corner spry — relay catching. The objective is for each team to complete the sequence of catches before the opposing team. The ball is thrown underarm to each player in turn.

A variation is relay stopping. The ball is rolled to each player who uses the long barrier to stop the ball before returning it with an underarm throw.

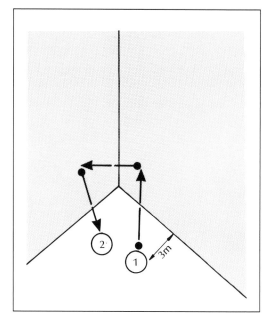

Drill 83

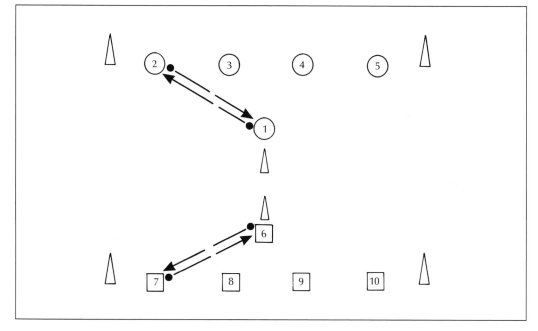

Drill 84

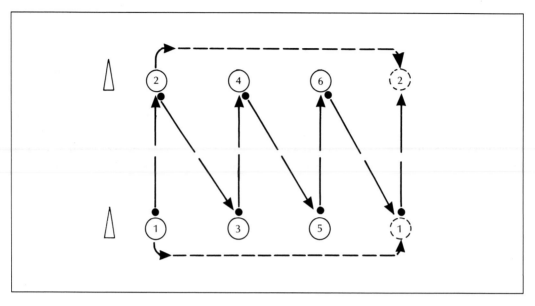

Drill 85

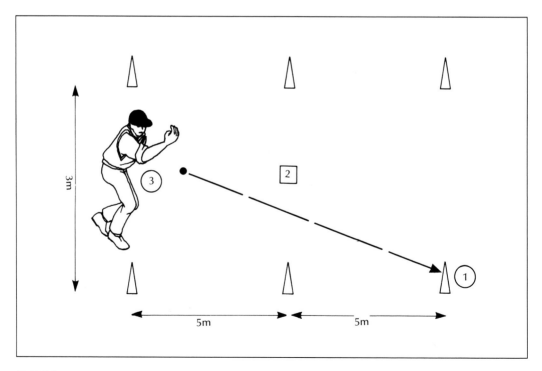

Drill 86

(85) Team spry — continuous catching. The ball is thrown underarm to the opposite player who returns it across to the next player before running to receive a catch at the end of the line.

This may be varied when the ball is thrown overarm for a catch at head height or rolled for practice in stopping using a short barrier.

(86) One against two catching competition. The objective is for fielders (1) and (3) to score goals by throwing the ball (underarm) past the middle fielder (2). The rules are:

— All players must remain on a line between the cones on either side.

— A goal is scored only when the ball passes below head height and above knee height between the middle cones.

— The centre player also scores one point for a stop and two points for a catch.

(87) Reflex catching. The ball is thrown for the batter (2) to give catches from forward and backward defensive strokes.

Variations in the delivery will enable the batter to direct the ball at different speeds to the fielders on both sides of the wicket.

(88) Head-height catching. The ball is thrown overarm or hit with a bat in a flat trajectory towards the fielder's head. Two or more fielders may be included, together with a wicket-keeper who collects the return throws.

Coaching Points

(i) The head is moved into the line of the ball.

(ii) The thumbs are touching, the palms facing the ball and fingers pointing upwards.

(iii) The catch is made with the hands close to the face.

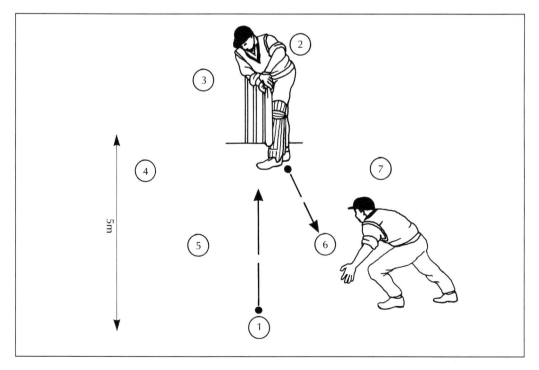

Drill 87

5m

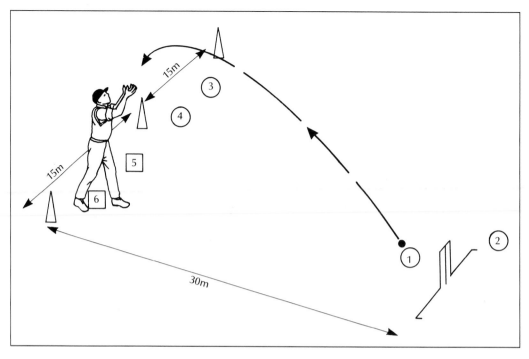

Drill 89

(89) High catching/boundary fielding. The ball is hit to each of the fielders in turn. They attempt to catch and quickly return the ball to the wicket-keeper. The practice may be made into a competition with the fielders divided into two teams, each trying to complete the most catches from a set number of deliveries.

The competition can progess, so that the ball is hit along the ground with each team of fielders trying to prevent it from crossing its own section of the boundary line between the skittles.

Coaching Points

(i)   The fielder moves quickly to the catching position underneath the ball.

(ii)   The head remains still and the eyes stay fixed on the ball.

(iii)   The hands come together with the palms facing upwards making a wide but relaxed target.

(iv)   The catch is made at eye-level with the hands and arms giving way to bring the ball on to the chest.

(90)   High catching over-the-head. The ball is hit with the bat or thrown high over the head of the fielder who turns and runs to take the catch. It is then returned quickly over the stumps to the wicket-keeper. The name of the fielder chosen to catch the ball is called by the batter before the ball is delivered.

Progressive difficulty can be introduced when the fielders stand facing away from the batter and have less time to see and judge the flight of the ball. A similar effect may be obtained when the ball is delivered from behind a sight screen.

(91)   Pressure catching. The ball is lobbed to a catchable height beyond one of the cones on the right or left side of the fielder (2). When the catch is made the ball is rolled immediately to the feeder (5) and the fielder quickly returns to the starting line between the cones in front of the bowler. Deliveries are continuous in

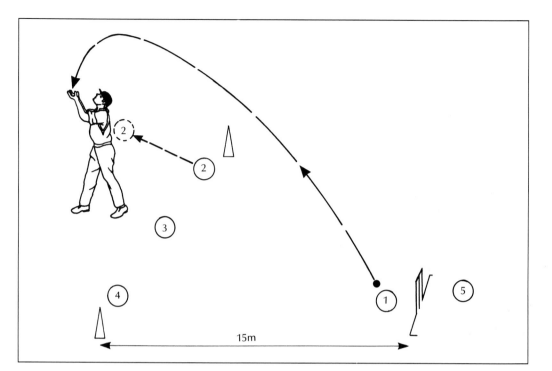

Drill 90

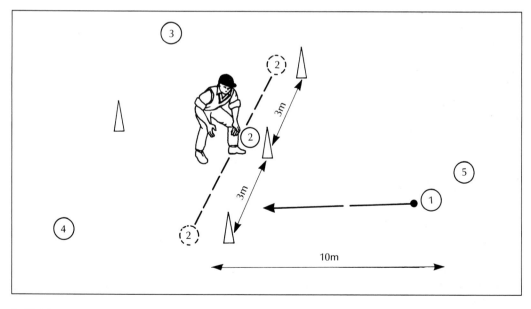

Drill 91

sets of six with just sufficient time between each to allow the fielder to return to the starting line. Fielders (3) and (4) retrieve the deliveries that are not stopped by the fielder. Both take their turns at catching.

(92) Rebound-catching relay. At the start of the race the first player in each team throws the ball at the wall and quickly runs to the back of the team. The second player moves in to catch the rebound, then passes it to the next player who repeats the throw from behind the 5m line. The sequence is continuous with one player throwing and the next catching until each has attempted both skills. The winning team is the first to complete the sequence.

COMPETITIONS

(93) Rotary cricket. The objective is for each individual to score as many runs as possible from a set number of deliveries. The rules are:
— Each player bowls and bats for one over of ten deliveries before moving to the next position in a clockwise rotation.
— Six runs are deducted from the score of a player who may be given out bowled, caught, stumped or run-out.

The positions are: (1) Padding-up; (2) Batter; (3) Wicket-keeper; (4) Un-padding; (5) Fielder; (6) Umpire; (7) Bowler; (8) Fielder; (9) Umpire.

(94) Continuous cricket. The rules are:
— The bowling (underarm) is continuous, irrespective of the position of the batter who may be dismissed by being bowled or caught.
— The incoming player remains seated, with the other members of the batting side, until the batter is out.
— A run is scored by running round the skittle (or chair) at fine-leg and returning to the crease.

(95) Pairs cricket. The rules are:
— A match consists of four overs, with each member of the bowling pair bowling one over to the opposing batting pair.
— An additional number of players, 5 to 10, are used as fielders and umpires.
— When one match has been completed a further two pairs compete in the next match while the players in the first match become fielders and umpires.

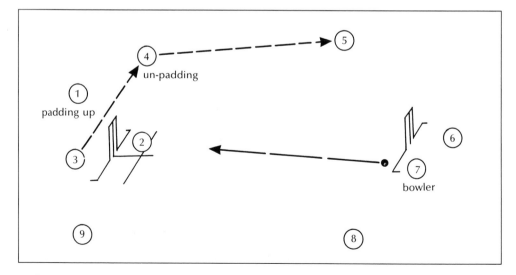

Drill 93

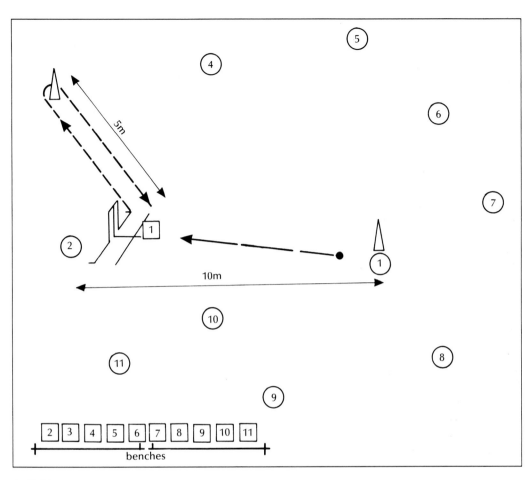

Drill 94

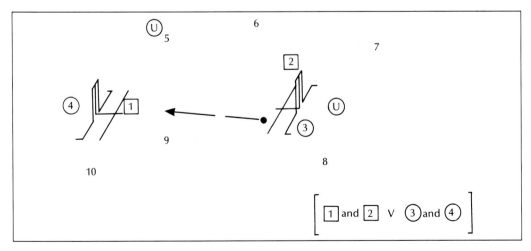

Drill 95

— The Laws of Cricket apply with the further exception that the winning pair in any match is the one with the highest average number of runs per wickets lost (i.e. runs scored divided by number of dismissals, with a bonus of 50 per cent of the runs scored added to the total when no wickets are lost).

(96)   6 a-side cricket. The Laws of Cricket apply with the following exceptions. Each team consists of six players, all of whom shall bat. Five of the fielding side bowl one over each, with one player keeping wicket. Two umpires are provided from the batting side.

Variations to the above can be introduced:
— The playing time may be extended by increasing the number of deliveries from each bowler.
— Other conditions may be applied to increase the scoring rate or encourage other aspects of the play.
— All wides and no-balls count as four runs.
— A batter scoring ten or more runs shall be retired.
— Any batter failing to score from three consecutive deliveries shall be deemed run-out.

(97)   Singles cricket. The rules are:
— The competition is played on a knock-out basis between individuals of similar ability.
— Each batter receives one over of ten deliveries from his/her opponent after which the positions are reversed until, after eight overs, each player has taken a turn at batting and bowling.
— In the next round of the competition the four winners play on the same basis. The two winners from this round then play in the final, both batting and bowling for two overs.
— The play is continuous throughout the sixteen overs of the competition. The fielders are the six players who are not directly involved in batting or bowling. The field placing is the responsibility of the bowler at that time.

— All the deliveries are made from the same end although the batter may be run-out at either end. When a run is scored the batter returns to the batting end to face the next delivery.
— A batter may be given out bowled, caught, lbw or run-out any number of times during the innings of ten deliveries. On each occasion, however, six runs are deducted from the score.

(98)   Stoolball. This game is more suitable for younger players as an introduction to cricket. The rules are:
— The ball is lobbed underarm (preferably by a teacher or coach) to waist height at full-pitch from the bowler's mark which is mid-way between the stumps. (The back of a chair above the seat is used as the wickets.)
— A run is scored when the batters cross and ground their bats behind the near legs of the chairs.
— A batter may be given out bowled, caught, or run-out.
— All players take a turn in batting and all are involved in fielding. The practice may be used to teach players the names of the fielding positions in addition to the skills of calling and running between the wickets.

(99)   8 a-side cricket. Before the match begins, each player is given a number and a card indicating the playing order. The Laws of Cricket apply with the following exceptions:
— Each team consists of eight players, with every player having a turn at batting and four from each team bowling (maximum three overs for each bowler).
— The team that scores the highest average number of runs per wickets lost is the winning team.
— The fielding side provides the wicket-keeper and seven fielders (including the bowlers).
— The batting side provides two fielders and two umpires, with two batters at the

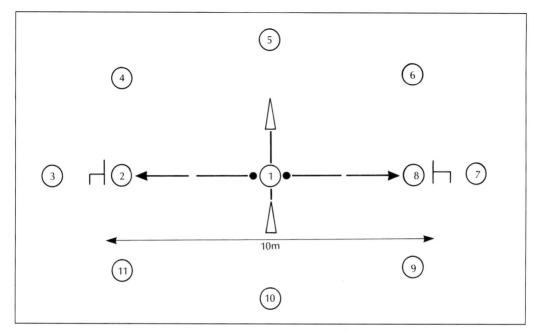

Drill 98

crease and two players padded-up. (In a competitive match, two independent umpires may be provided in place of the two members of the batting side.)

— Each pair of batters receives a total of eighteen deliveries from three overs, and change after the third, sixth and ninth

over (the batting side receives a total of twelve overs).

— When a pair of batters complete their innings without losing a wicket, a bonus of 50 per cent of their total runs is added to the score.

	Batters	Padding up	Fielders	Umpires
To begin	1 & 2	3 & 4	5 & 6	7 & 8
At the end of the 3rd over	3 & 4	5 & 6	7 & 8	1 & 2
At the end of the 6th over	5 & 6	7 & 8	1 & 2	3 & 4
At the end of the 9th over	7 & 8	–	3 & 4	5 & 6

During the final three overs, players 1 and 2 are off the field.

Drill 99

(100)   Conditioned games. At the start of a game, various conditions may be applied to direct and concentrate the practice on particular objectives. These should be explained and demonstrated at the outset. They should encourage continuity of play and involve minimal changes to the Laws of Cricket.

Examples of conditioned games:

—   Limited overs. The objective is to enable a match to be completed within a limited time.

—   A specified number of bowlers to be used by each team (e.g. six bowlers with a maximum of four overs for each bowler). The objective is to increase the number of bowlers participating in the game.

—   Limited number of overs to be played by any pair of batters. The objective is to distribute the opportunity for batting practice more equally between players.

—   Restrictions in the placing of fielders. The objective is to encourage practice of certain types of batting strokes.

—   Environmental or local conditions (e.g. for indoor or other restricted playing areas). The objective is to enable the Laws of Cricket to be applied as near as possible under the restricted playing conditions (e.g. six runs may be scored from a direct hit to the wall behind the bowler).

—   A batter may be given out for failing to score from three consecutive deliveries. The objective is to encourage a faster scoring rate.

—   Individual scoring targets (e.g. a batter may be given a target to score a certain number of runs from a set number of deliveries). The objective is to encourage a change in batting tactics.

—   Individual or team penalties (e.g. four runs are added to the batting score for a wide or for a delivery outside the leg stump). The objective is to encourage greater accuracy in bowling.

2 Physical Fitness

The constant rise in standards in sport can be attributed to many things, such as improved techniques and equipment. However, in some sports the equipment is relatively unimportant and the techniques may not have changed much. What, then, can account for improvement in such sports? Quite probably the key factor is physical fitness. Not only does physical fitness contribute to the end result in cricket (to whatever extent), but it is now also recognised as a very important part of training. Indeed, fitness is important at all levels of cricket because while it is essential for international competition, it is also beneficial for beginners, improving both their effectiveness and enjoyment of the game.

WHAT IS PHYSICAL FITNESS?

Physical fitness involves a multitude of components, so making it difficult to refer to fitness as one single thing. In fact when people ask how 'fit' you are, they are asking a rather naive question. If someone asked me the same type of question about my car, I might say that the car is excellent for comfort, good on motorways, not very good for acceleration and in need of improvement when starting in the wet! An overall comment on how 'good' ('fit') my car is depends on which aspect you are referring to.

Similarly, we can refer to many different parts, or components, of fitness. Nowadays there is a great deal of interest in fitness for health, which includes exercises for stamina (e.g. jogging), posture, weight control, etc. However, fitness for sport will include some of these components as well as others, such as speed and power. The importance of each

component for your sport obviously depends on the sport itself. Cricket is a game requiring most types of fitness at some time. However, you can imagine the marathon runner and weight-lifter, for example, having – for the most part – quite different fitness training programmes.

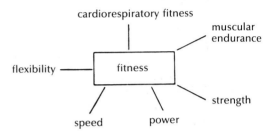

Fig 1   A model of physical fitness for sport.

The components of physical fitness for sport which require physical training are summarised in Fig 1. As you can see, these components are cardiorespiratory fitness (stamina), muscular endurance, strength, power, speed, and flexibility. Many years ago sports coaches used to refer to the main components of fitness as the 'six Ss': stamina, strength, speed, suppleness, skill and (p)sychology!

One could easily add to these six, mental fitness, diet and nutrition, injury prevention and those other areas illustrated in Fig 1. The latter shows the main components of fitness requiring physical activity and changes in the physiological state of the body. (Some of these other areas are dealt with in other chapters of this book.)

One final point on the definition of fitness; some people say that fitness is a set of attributes that individuals have or achieve and which help them in their ability to perform physical activity.

The phrase 'have or achieve' is an interesting one since it suggests that fitness in sport is dependent on two things: natural ability ('have') and training ('achieve'). Many aspects of fitness are governed by our heredity, yet with training we are able to make the most of what we have. Unfortunately, 750cc Fiats will never become Formula One competitors. However, you could enjoy being a good 750cc Fiat given the right care and attention, especially if you race cars of the same type! Indeed, with good maintenance (training) the 750cc Fiat will be able to beat a less well maintained car with a larger engine and may possess other qualities than just power.

PRINCIPLES OF FITNESS TRAINING

Regardless of the component of fitness we are talking about, there are certain basic principles that apply to all aspects of fitness training in cricket. These are:

(i)   frequency
(ii)   intensity
(iii)   progressive overload
(iv)   time
(v)   type (of exercise)
(vi)   specificity
(vii)   reversibility

Frequency

Frequency refers to the number of training sessions during a particular time period. It is usual to speak of frequency in terms of sessions in a week. Most sports require 2 to 3 sessions per week, although obviously those people striving for the highest honours will train much more frequently. (Indeed, many sports today require their top athletes to train

several times a day!) However, for most people, significant fitness improvements can be made with about three sessions per week.

Intensity

This refers to how hard one should train. This will differ greatly between individuals, although similar training programmes can be performed on a relative basis. This means, for example, that the same two athletes can perform three sets of five repetitions of the leg-press exercise in the weight-training room at 75 per cent of their maximum. However, the actual weight lifted may differ considerably.

Superior athletes with an extensive training background are also likely to be able to train at a higher level for longer and recover more quickly. The intensity of your training will have a major bearing on its effectiveness. Too little intensity will not produce much of an effect, and too much intensity is likely to lead

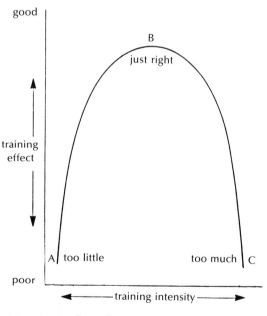

Note A→B effect of progressive overload.

Fig 2   Progressive overload.

to injury and fatigue. For these reasons, the principle of progressive overload is important (*see* Fig 2).

Progressive Overload

The old story of Milo carrying a calf on his shoulders is the perfect illustration of progressive overload. Milo started off carrying a small calf but as the animal grew in size and weight, Milo did not find it progressively more difficult to carry. Instead, he adapted to the increasing load as his muscles grew stronger. Eventually, he could carry a fully-grown bull. Two things are important here: first, Milo was *progressive* in his 'training'. He gradually adapted to the increasing load. Imagine what would have happened if Milo had tried to lift the bull having had several months of inactivity! Second, Milo adapted to the load through *overload*. This is a fundamental mechanism since, with increased training, the body will adapt and grow (with sensible progressive overload) or collapse (through inappropriate training – 'too much too soon') (*see* Fig 2).

Time

This simply refers to the amount of time spent in a training session. Time spent thus will vary greatly depending on the sport and the individual. Most fitness training sessions, allowing for adequate warm-up and cool-down, last upwards of 40 minutes.

Type (of Exercise)

Fitness training sessions will vary in terms of type of exercise. Some sessions will contain predominantly cardiorespiratory exercises, others strength and flexibility, etc. This will depend, again, on the individual and the sport in question. For example, the fitness requirements of the wicket-keeper will clearly differ from the specialist fast bowler.

You may have noticed that the above concepts can be easily remembered by using the word 'FITT': frequency, intensity (including overload), time and type.

This 'FITT principle' forms the corner-stone for many sports' fitness-training programmes (*see* Fig 6). However, there are other basic principles to remember.

Specificity

Your fitness training must be geared to making you a better cricketer. It may be very satisfying to improve your best time for your favourite 5km running course, but if it doesn't help your cricket it is misplaced effort. Your fitness training, therefore, should be specific to the sport. However, this does not mean that the fundamental components of fitness are ignored. It would be pointless to train for hours every day to improve your throwing accuracy on the run and at the same time ignore developing your running speed to get to the ball! A combination of factors is therefore required.

Reversibility

'Use it or lose it!' is a common expression in sport. Unless you continue training, the fitness you have built up will quickly be lost. Some people seem to 'retain' their fitness better than others but what occurs here is that the individuals concerned are likely to have a high natural ability to perform, as mentioned earlier. They will still lose the effects of training if they fail to continue, but the effects may not appear to be so marked. A run-down Formula One car will still beat a well-tuned 750cc Fiat!

COMPONENTS OF FITNESS FOR CRICKET

Cricket is a game requiring players to develop a number of fitness qualities as each is likely to be required at sometime in the game (*see* Fig 3). However, some of these components

Fitness components		Not very Important	Useful	Important	Very important
Cardiorespiratory Fitness			*		
Muscular Endurance				*	
Strength				*	
Power				*	
Speed (and agility)					*
Flexibility				*	

Fig 3   Fitness components for cricket.

are considered more important in cricket than others. Fig 3 gives a guide as to the relative importance of each of the fitness components for cricket. The purpose of this section of the chapter, therefore, is to outline each of these components and show how they can be developed to maximise their effectiveness in the game. Before these components are dealt with, it is important to say something about the warm-up.

Warm-Up

This is an important period of exercise performed prior to the main part of the training session or game and is used to prepare the body for vigorous action. The warm-up can be divided into two main phases: general warm-up and sport-specific warm-up.

General Warm-Up

This should consist of the following:

(i) Gentle rhythmic 'total body' exercises, such as jogging or callisthenics which should slowly increase in intensity and produce a slight sweat and raised pulse.
(ii) Static stretching exercises (see 'Flexibility' later in this chapter).

Sport-Specific Warm-Up

Part of the warm-up, as the name suggests, should include exercises which specifically prepare you for your game, such as leg stretches for wicket-keepers, arm and shoulder stretches for bowlers etc. These can then be followed by practices designed for the skills themselves. (The warm-up process for cricket is summarised in Fig 4.)

In addition to preparing to start activity, you should also prepare to finish! This is done by cooling-down after periods of vigorous activity with similar exercises to those used in the warm-up, such as gentle rhythmic exercises and stretching. In fact, this is a particularly good time for stretching as your muscles will be warm and hence very receptive to this form of exercise.

CARDIORESPIRATORY (STAMINA) FITNESS

Let us first try to understand the terminology! Cardiorespiratory fitness can also be known as cardiovascular fitness, aerobic exercise, stamina fitness, and probably a host of other names. For our purposes cardiorespiratory fitness, or CR, is probably good enough.

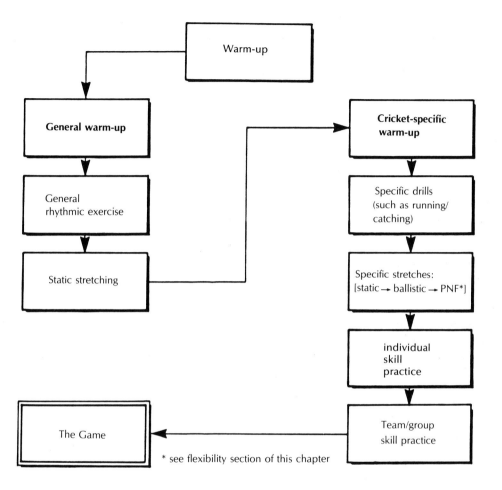

Fig 4   The warm-up process for cricket.

To help you remember this: CR is the stamina-type fitness associated with activities such as cycling, jogging and swimming. The local muscular endurance fitness needed in exercises like sit-ups or press-ups is, of course, very much related to cardiorespiratory fitness since it is the CR system that is responsible for getting oxygen to the working muscles. However, specific local muscular endurance will be dealt with separately since a whole set of different exercises can be prescribed for that component.

Physiologists have known for a long time that the body operates through different types of 'energy systems'. For example, the fast bowler requires short bursts of high-intensity effort whereas the slower bowlers may need a more prolonged effort (i.e. a greater number of overs) often at a lower intensity.

The three main energy systems are summarised in Fig 5, which shows CR fitness, or stamina, is associated with the 'aerobic' energy system. The word aerobic means 'with air' (or oxygen) and refers to continuous activities

ENERGY SYSTEMS			
	1	**2**	**3**
Duration	0–15 secs	15 secs–2 mins	Over 2 mins
Technical term	ATP–PC system	LA (lactic acid)	Aerobic system
Description	Strength, power, speed	Short-term muscular endurance	Long-term muscular endurance and aerobic activity
Cricket activities	Quick single	More prolonged running in field or at wicket	Recovery between plays

ATP = adenosine triphosphate
PC = phosphocreatine

Fig 5   The main energy systems of the body and their practical meaning in cricket.

whereby the oxygen that is breathed in is sufficient to supply the energy required for that particular activity. That is why walking is aerobic and sprinting is 'anaerobic' (without oxygen/air), as high-speed sprinting cannot be sustained for long (*see* Fig 5). (Anaerobic training is covered in more detail later in this chapter.)

Aerobic Endurance

Aerobic CR fitness is developed by progressively taxing the CR system (i.e. heart, lungs, blood vessels, blood). The most practical indication of aerobic training intensity, therefore, is the heart rate, or pulse. It is generally thought that gains in CR fitness will occur when the heart rate (HR) is raised to a sufficient level for a 'training effect'. But what is a sufficient level? As a general rule optimal gains in CR fitness occur when the HR is raised to within 60 to 90 per cent of maximum, where maximum is estimated as 220 minus your age (in years). This figure gives the number of beats per minute. For example:

Person: A. Robic
Age: 20 years
Estimated maximum HR:
220–20   = 200 beats per minute (bpm)
Training zone = 60–90 of max
                      = 120–180 bpm

This is likely to yield a conservative estimate at the lower end of the range for most active sportspeople, so another, and simpler, method is to add 25 to your age and subtract the sum from 220. For example:

Person: A. Robic
Age: 20 years
CR training intensity
= 220–(20+25)
= 220–45
= 175 bpm

To actually count your own pulse, you can use either your wrist or neck. At the wrist (the 'radial pulse') simply place three fingers (not your thumb) lightly on your up-turned wrist at the base of the thumb. It is probably easier to count for fifteen seconds and then multiply by four for your bpm figure. Errors will occur but

FITT component	Minimum criteria
Frequency	3 times per week
Intensity	Elevated heart rate between 60–90% of maximum, or 220–(age +25) beats per minute
Time	20 minutes
Type (of exercise)	Gross body exercise, such as running, swimming, cycling.

Fig 6   The FITT principle as applied to cardiorespiratory training.

these should diminish with practice. A stronger pulse can be felt at the neck (the 'carotid pulse') by placing the fingers gently against the neck at the base of the angle of the jaw bone. For reasons of safety, don't press too hard.

The FITT principle for aerobic fitness training is summarised in Fig 6. This shows minimum criteria and many active sportspeople will require greater levels of training. Also, for maximum benefit in the game of cricket, the type of exercise used should be as relevant and similar to the game as possible. This suggests that swimming and cycling will not be as good for the cricketer as running, and indeed running might best be done in 'interval' form to simulate the 'stop-start' action of the game itself. However, it is important to remember that the CR system is central to recovery from all forms of exercise, so although some players need not have the running endurance of the long-distance athlete, they do need a fundamental base of adequate aerobic fitness.

The practices described in Chapter 1 could be incorporated into aerobic fitness training and these can be useful for several reasons:

(i)   They provide a game-relevant form of training.
(ii)   Players can immediately see the point of the activities.
(iii)   They allow for variety in fitness training.

However, caution needs to be exercised in that the load placed on the player should not be so great that the skills are performed badly. Fatigue is a major cause of skill breakdown.

Assessing Aerobic Fitness

The best way to use tests of fitness is to compare scores over time for the same player. In other words, use tests to track progress. Simple 'field' tests can be used, such as recording the distance run around a track in 12 minutes, the time taken to run 2.5km, etc. Assuming that the conditions stay the same from one test to the next, including motivation of the player, then changes in scores will give some indication of changing fitness levels. Another simple indication is to step up and down on a bench or stair approximately 50cm high (although the exact height does not really matter). Perform for a set time (e.g. five minutes), to a definite rhythm or beat (such as on a record) and then take your pulse. If this exercise is repeated at a later date in exactly the same way (i.e. same time, height of step, beat), changes in the pulse give some indication of CR fitness changes (assuming, of course, you can accurately take your own pulse). Such simple methods can be appealing but they are only rough guides to progress. With the increasing availability of laboratory testing, more valid measures should be possible for a greater number of players.

Term	Definition
Strength	The maximum force that a muscle, or group of muscles, can generate. Sometimes the statement 'at a specified speed or velocity' can be added to this definition because force will diminish as the speed of the limb increases.
Muscular endurance	The ability of the muscle or muscle group to continue applying force.
Power	The product of force and velocity; in simpler terms, strength x speed.
Flexibility	Range of motion about a joint or series of joints.

Fig 7   Definition of terms applied to muscle fitness.

Convincing the Sceptics

It is quite likely that many players and coaches will doubt the real value of CR fitness for cricket. However, while it is not the most important of the fitness components (and is certainly less important in cricket than in, say, rugby union) it is still a component of fitness that is increasingly important in the modern game. This is, of course, particularly true for the faster one-day game where fitness between the wickets and in the field may win or lose the game. It is perfectly acceptable for the 'social' cricketer to place less emphasis on this type of fitness training, but players aspiring to the top level cannot afford to omit CR fitness training from their plan.

MUSCULAR ENDURANCE

Before proceeding with 'muscle fitness' you should check Fig 7, for a definition of the terms used and to note that the different components are often interrelated — for example, to develop power both strength and speed are necessary. In this section we consider the components separately but, obviously, they overlap in reality.

Muscular endurance follows naturally from aerobic fitness. Since muscular endurance is the ability to repeat muscle contractions over time, such as repetition sit-ups, improving this component of fitness requires relatively high numbers of repetitions to be performed. (This is the reverse of strength development, as explained later. *See also* Fig 8.) It is clearly the case that large numbers of repetitions can only be performed with a relatively small resistance. While this could be external resistance, such as weights, it is often sufficient just to use body-weight, such as in press-ups and sit-ups. (A series of basic body-weight endurance exercises is shown in Figs 9 and 10.)

More specific application to cricket can be made by constant repetition of certain game skills. However, care should be taken that

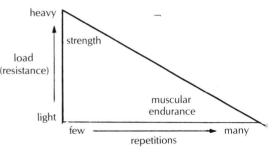

Fig 8   The strength-muscular endurance continuum.

Name	Figure	Muscle action
Press-ups	11(i)	Back of upper arms (triceps) and chest.
Pull-ups [2]	11(ii)	Front of upper arms (biceps), shoulders and upper back
Sit-ups [3]	11(iii)	Stomach
Back extensions [4]	11(iv)	Back muscles

Note: leg muscles may require additional resistance. (*See* the leg exercises shown in the weight-training section of this chapter). People sometimes refer to 'pull-ups' (2) as involving an overgrasp grip and 'chins' an undergrasp grip. The effect is similar. You should always perform sit-ups (3) with bent legs and for back extensions (4) you should not lift your shoulders far above your hips.

Fig 9   Basic body-weight muscular endurance exercises.

Fig 10   Muscular endurance exercises (i) Press-ups. (ii) Pull-ups. (iii) Sit-ups. (iv) Back extensions.

the skills are exactly replicated. (*See* 'Strength and Power' section for some cricket-related exercises.)

Assessing Muscular Endurance

Basic tests of muscular endurance are simple to perform, although always dependent on the subject performing at maximum effort and motivation. As with the CR tests, use them to plot individual progress. Any muscular endurance exercise can be used as a test as long as it can easily be scored. For example, one test could be the number of sit-ups performed in a set time (e.g. 1 minute). However, comparisons are only valid if the techniques are always the same.

STRENGTH AND POWER

No other area of physical fitness has suffered more than strength training from misunderstanding and mythology. The 'circus strongman' image still persists in many instances, but it is just as easy to find slim 800m runners lifting weights as is it 125kg shot-putters! Weight training, the most common of strength-training methods, is simply a way of increasing the resistance placed on the muscles to stimulate their growth and development. While on this subject, some popular misconceptions need correction: women will *not* become masculine if they lift weights; it is not possible for muscle to turn into fat; weight training will not slow you down! Indeed modern-day athletes use strength and power training extensively, although it must be said that some sports are more advanced in their methods than others. In short, there is no dynamic sport where some form of resistance training is not required – including cricket!

Before proceeding, it is worth looking again at Fig 8. Very few sports involve maximum force at slow speeds and most require 'fast strength' — i.e. power. However, because power is a combination of strength and speed, the two terms will be dealt with together. Pure speed will be dealt with separately.

Without going into great detail on how muscles actually work, it is worth noting briefly that there are different types of muscle fibre. 'Slow-twitch' (ST or type I) fibres, as their name suggests, are endurance fibres with low power. The 'fast-twitch' (FT or type II) fibres are the opposite – powerful but only able to operate briefly. In fact, there are type IIa fibres and IIb fibres, the latter being the very fast-twitch action and IIa fibres, being fast-twitch but with some endurance capacity.

We all possess both ST and FT fibres in varying proportions, and this is due to heredity. However, through a process of self-selection, it is likely that, for example, marathon runners will have a high percentage of ST fibres and sprinters (and fast bowlers) a high percentage of FT Fibres. Great variability within these extreme groups probably exists. Fig 11 summarises the differences between the two main types of fibres, and Fig 12 illustrates the order in which the fibres are always recruited.

This order (Type I, then IIa, then IIb), and the associated intensity of exercise to bring about this recruitment, tells us that heavy resistance and high intensity training (high loads with repetitions of six or less) may well be a very good way to develop explosive strength. This often contradicts the commonly held belief that heavy resistance training will 'slow you down'. Once repetitions start to exceed about six, the initial tension on the muscle may be reduced and less Type IIb fibres will be recruited. However, fast movements with lower resistances can be used to recruit FT fibres — such as during movements of fast velocity but with a lighter weight. In short, exercise must be of an intense nature to recruit FT fibres, and this can include heavy resistance work previously thought to be detrimental for games players (see Fleck and Kraemer, 1987).

Characteristics	Slow Twitch	Fast Twitch
Aerobic capacity	High	Low
Anaerobic capacity	Low	High
Contraction time	Slow	Fast
Force	Low	High
Activities	Endurance-type	Sprint/explosive-type
Fatigue	Slow	Fast

Fig 11   Summary of characteristics of fast-and-slow-twitch muscle fibres, adapted from Fox, E.L. Sports Physiology (Saunders College, 1979).

Types of Strength and Power Training Methods

There are several different ways of exercising for strength. These are:

(i) 'Constant resistance' (sometimes called isotonic). This is the conventional type of training involving barbells, dumb-bells and body weight. Although called constant resistance, this is slightly inaccurate as the actual resistance on the muscle will change as the body levers create different forces. The weight on

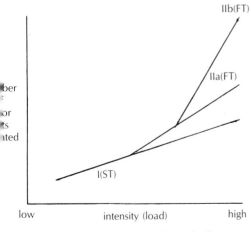

Fig 12   Recruitment pattern of muscle fibres.

the bar, however, does remain the same. This is probably the most accessible form of effective strength training for cricket players.
(ii) 'Static resistance' (isometric). Here, force is applied to an immovable object and so no movement is observed. This is not a very useful form of training for cricketers because of its static nature. This type of training, too, can also be unsafe for older people as it can create a sharp rise in blood pressure.
(iii) 'Same-speed' training (isokinetic). Performed with the aid of a machine which will only allow the limb to move at a set speed, the resistance on the muscle depends on the voluntary effort of the athlete. This form of training has some benefits for water sports enthusiasts and can be seen to be used with special machines, such as isokinetic swim benches, but is less relevant to cricket.
(iv) 'Variable resistance'. A form of exercise performed on machines which vary the resistance put on the muscle through its range of movement. This helps overcome the inherent weakness of isotonic training whereby the muscle is only working at maximal force in one part of the range of movement. However, variable resistance machines are still not readily available to all athletes and tend only to cater for single-joint actions. Since most sports movements are multi-jointed in their action, a

combination of isotonic and variable exercise is warranted (*see* Fleck and Kraemer, 1987).

Obviously, exercises can be divided up into body parts such as lower, middle and upper. However, in addition to this it is worth splitting the exercises into three types according to their function:

— general
— specific to cricket
— competition-specific

General strength/power exercises are those nearly all sportspeople require for basic increases in strength and power in the major muscle groups of the body.

Specific exercises are those which work the muscles particularly relevant to the sport in question – i.e. cricket.

Competition-specific exercises are those resistance exercises which copy, as closely as possible, the actual sports skill. For example, exercises for cricketers might include pulley resistance exercises to simulate the bowling action, or a single-arm upright rowing action as in the follow through with the bat. Figs 13–34 suggest some resistance exercises for each of these categories and explain exactly how the exercises should be performed.

Figure	Exercise	Major muscles involved	Equipment
16	Power clean	Hips, legs, back (power development)	Barbell
17	Front squat	Hips, legs (quadriceps)	Barbell
18	Leg extension	Quadriceps	Machine
19	Leg curl	Hamstrings	Machine
20	Side bends	Oblique (side) abdominals	Dumb-bell
21	Bench press	Chest, triceps, shoulders	Barbell or Machine
22	Arm curl	Biceps	Barbell or Machine

Fig 13   General resistance exercises for cricketers.

Fig 14   Power clean.

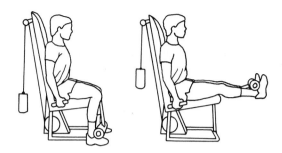

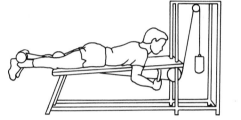

Fig 16   Leg extension.

Fig 15   Front squat.

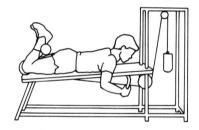

Fig 17   Leg Curl.

Fig 18   Side Bends.

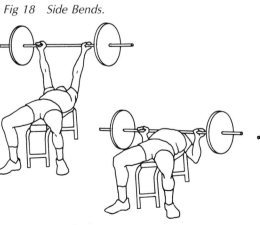

Fig 19   Bench press.

Fig 20   Arm curls.

Figure	Exercise	Starting position	Movement	Other points
17	Power clean	Feet under bar, hip-width apart. Shoulder-width overgrasp grip. Hips below shoulders. Arms straight, back flat.	Lift bar from floor with straight arms and keep back flat. Extend body. Keep bar close in. Turn wrists over and receive bar on front of shoulders. Bend legs to receive bar. Lower to thighs, then to floor.	Have bar 20 cm off the floor to begin. Use blocks or wooden disks for this. Make movement smooth and, later, fast and dynamic.
18	Front squat	Bar on chest, high elbows. Feet flat just outside hip-width.	Squat under control to 'thighs parallel'. Return to standing. Keep chest up throughout.	Avoid deep squatting.
19	Leg extension	Feet under lower pads. Sit upright.	Extend leg then lower under control.	
20	Leg curl	Face down on machine, heels under top pads.	Bring heels up towards buttocks. Return under control.	
21	Side bends	Stand with feet beyond hip-width. Dumb-bell in one hand at the side, other hand behind head or at the side.	Bend sideways with weight, return to middle position and beyond to position of stretch. Return to start.	Move sideways only. Do not use a dumb-bell in each hand.
22	Bench press	Lie face up on a bench. Hips, shoulders, head all on bench. Shoulder-width grip of bar.	Lower bar to chest. Extend arms to straighten them fully.	If using a barbell rather than machine, beginners may find it easier to balance if they start to exercise with the bar on the chest.
23	Arm curl	Undergrasp grip on bar; upright body.	Pull bar to top of the chest, keeping elbows at the side of the body. Return under control.	

Note: Although specific breathing techniques can be recommended for each exercise, it is often easier, particularly with beginners, simply to suggest that they breathe freely and naturally. Do *not* hold your breath during the execution of these exercises. This applies to all the exercises in Figs 17–32.

Fig 21 Explanation of general weight-training exercises.

Figure	Exercise	Major muscles involved	Equipment
23	Split squats	Quadriceps (and for hip flexibility)	Barbell
24	Single-arm cheat rowing	Trunk rotators	Dumb-bell
25	Upright rowing	Deltoids and biceps	Barbell or machine
26	Wrist roller	Forearms	Machine
27	Latissimus pulldown	Latissimus dorsi, biceps and upper back	Pulldown machine
28	Straight-arm pullovers	Chest and latissimus dorsi	Barbell
29	Bent-arm pullovers	Chest and latissimus dorsi	Barbell

Fig 22   Specific resistance exercises for cricketers.

Fig 23   Split Squats.

Fig 24   Single-arm chest rowing.

Fig 26   Wrist roller.

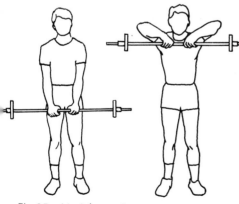

Fig 25   Upright rowing.

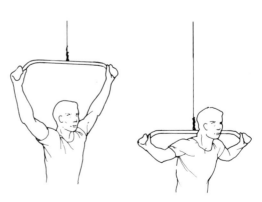

Fig 27   Latissimus pulldown.

73

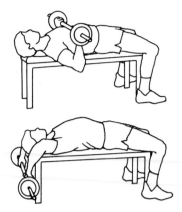

Fig 29   Bent-arm pullovers.

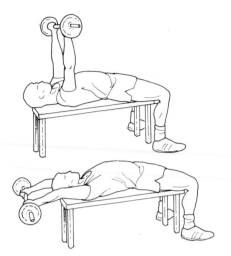

Fig 28   Straight-arm pullovers.

Figure	Exercise	Starting position	Movement	Other points
23	Split squat	Bar on front shoulders, elbows high. Feet split front–back. Front foot flat, toes pointing slightly inwards. Rear foot on toes, pointing forwards.	Bend front leg and push hips down and forward. Maintain upright trunk. Push back off front leg once thigh is parallel to floor.	Repeat exercise with other foot forwards.
24	Single-arm cheat rowing	Bend forward and support one arm on a bench. With the other arm, lift dumb-bell. Feet split front and back.	Lift the dumb-bell and rotate the trunk so that the chest faces away from the bench.	
25	Upright rowing	Stand upright; narrow overgrasp grip with bar at thighs.	Pull the bar to chin level, keeping elbows high. Return under control.	
26	Wrist roller	Grip roller.	Roll weight up and then roll it back down.	
27	Latissimus pull-down	Wide overgrasp grip of pulley bar. Kneel down.	Pull bar to base of neck. Return under control.	
28	Straight-arm pullovers	Lying on back, on a bench; bar held at shoulder·width, arm's length above chest.	Lower bar backwards until bar just passes line of the body. Pull back to start position.	Perform the first few repetitions in stages to avoid overstretching.
29	Bent-arm pull-overs	Lying on back, on a bench; bar held on chest with shoulder-width grip.	Move bar back over face and down below head level. Pull back to start position.	Keep elbows in towards the middle of the body.

Fig 30   Explanation of specific weight-training exercises.

Figure	Exercise	Major muscles involved	Simulation of	Equipment
30	Bowling pulley	Shoulders, chest, latissimus dorsi and trunk	Bowling	Pulley
31	Single-arm upright rowing	Deltoid biceps	Batting follow-through	Dumb-bell or machine

Fig 31   Competition-specific resistance exercises for cricketers.

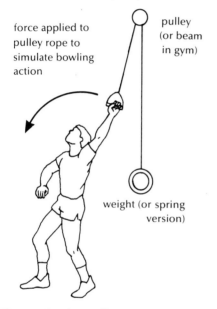

force applied to pulley rope to simulate bowling action

pulley (or beam in gym)

weight (or spring version)

Fig 32   Bowling pulley.

Fig 33   Single-arm upright rowing.

Figure	Exercise	Starting position	Movement	Other points
30	Bowling pulley	Action requires direct simulation of bowling action against pulley resistance.		Keep good technique throughout.
31	Single-arm up-right rowing	Stand upright with overgrasp grip on dumb-bell or machine.	Pull weight to chin level with a high elbow. Lower under control.	Work both arms consecutively.

Fig 34   Explanation of competition-specific resistance exercises.

A powerful drive off the back foot by Allan Border (Australia). Strength training is an important part of the development of a top-class cricketer.

	TIME		
	Preparation phase (out of season)	**Pre-competitive phase (pre-season)**	**Competitive phase (during season)**
Emphasis	Strength	Power	Maintenance
Loading (intensity)	High	High	Medium
Exercises	Mainly general	General plus specific (some competition-specific)	Mainly specific and competition-specific
Frequency	2–3 times per week	2–3 times per week	2 times per week
Time (excluding warm-up and cool-down)	45–60mins	40mins	30mins

Fig 35   Developing strength and power across the training year.

Planning Strength and Power Training

It should always be remembered that strength and power training is merely an aid to improved performance in cricket. Training should therefore be 'cycled' so that the maximum benefits are derived. This can be a complex matter, but space permits only a brief discussion here.

Basically, the strength and power training should develop across three phases of the year, starting at the end of the season and after a brief rest. The player should start a basic strength programme. This will include mostly exercises from Fig 13. As the season approaches, the training should become more dynamic and specific to the game. Hence, exercises from Fig 22 can now be added, along with the competition-specific exercises the closer the season gets. In the season itself, the number of sessions may be reduced say from three to two, as the aim is to maintain the increased strength and power gained in the previous periods. This process is shown in Fig 35.

Using part of the FITT principle, the following guidelines can be offered to vary the training according to the individual.

Beginner (with weight training)

Frequency:	2–3 times per week.
Intensity:	low; all weights should be light enough to perform 8–10 repetitions in good style, 3 sets each exercise.
Time:	initially short (30 min), could increase to 45 min.

Intermediate

Frequency:	2–3 times per week.
Intensity:	medium, occasionally high. Last few repetitions should be fairly hard (5 sets of repetitions).
Time:	up to 45 min.

Advanced

Frequency:	3–4 times per week.
Intensity:	varied, including *occasional* maximums.
Time:	45 min–1 hour. This would only be required by players needing higher levels of strength and power, such as fast bowlers and higher order specialist batters.

The structure of each session should be:

(i)   warm-up
(ii)   general exercises
(iii)   specific/competition-specific exercises
(iv)   cool-down

Needs Assessment

In their excellent book *Designing Resistance Training Programmes,* (1987) Fleck and Kraemer list a variety of important factors that should be assessed in planning a strength and power training programme for an athlete. The three major 'needs assessment' categories identified were: exercise movements, metabolism used, injury prevention.

Exercise Movements: The coach, in planning the strength/power programmes of the players, needs to know: which specific muscles and muscle groups need to be emphasised; are there any specific joint angles that need strengthening; what should the emphasis be in terms of strength, power, endurance, etc; and, finally, which type of exercise(s) should be used (i.e. isotonic, isometric, isokinetic, etc)? This requires the cricket coach to be familiar with fitness training principles and basic biomechanics and anatomy.

Metabolism used: What is the estimated percentage contribution from each of the three main energy systems outlined in Fig 5?

Injury prevention: Develop the most common sites of possible injury and select exercises suitable for sites of previous injuries.

Most of these factors require specialist weight-training coaches working in close co-operation with informed cricket coaches.

Assessing Strength and Power

Assessing strength and power is often recommended by coaches and fitness experts. However, the assessment of strength can be a problem, particularly for beginners who are unused to maximum muscular effort. This could be a dangerous form of exercise. Also, some exercises require considerable skill learning prior to one repetition maximums being attempted. Although safer forms of strength testing, such as grip-strength tests, can be performed, they are of limited value in most sports contexts, although probably more useful to cricket than to many sports. However, it would appear to be more advantageous to assess power and, in the case of cricket, power relevant to a particular skill, such as speed off the mark at the crease, or speed in throwing.

Additional Considerations in Strength and Power Training

Safety

Weight-training has an excellent safety record compared with many other sports and activities. This is particularly the case when weight trainers lift in a well-planned environment with good supervision. Nevertheless, like most activities, a safety code should be adhered to. The main points to note are:

(i) Personal safety:
—   Learn correct techniques.
—   Train with other people so they can help out.
—   Warm up properly.

Improvised but effective. Gordon Greenidge (West Indies) demonstrates an alert mind and a good sense of balance in hitting a boundary.

— Wear appropriate clothing, including training shoes.
— Progress gradually through a planned schedule.

(ii) External safety:
— Check all apparatus before use.
— Keep all apparatus well maintained and clean.
— Have floor space free of obstacles, such as loose disks.
— Plan the floor space for maximum, but safe, use.
— Determine the maximum number of people who can safely use the facility, and then stick to it.

Children

It is always tempting when encouraging youngsters into sport to give them the same training programme as adults. This would be a mistake, and in particular for strength/power exercises. It is generally recommended that pre-pubertal children should not lift heavy weights, although light exercises are unlikely to cause harm. Depending on the child's development, around the age of 13 to 14 years is probably suitable for starting weight-training where the emphasis would be on technique and skill learning under qualified supervision.

SPEED TRAINING

The cricketer who has conscientiously trained with resistance exercises, especially the power exercises like the power clean (Fig 14) should find that their overall movement speed has improved.

However, there are different types of speed in sport. The ability to react quickly to a stimulus is called 'reaction time' and is best illustrated in cricket by the reaction of the player batting against a fast bowler. (Reaction time here is the time between the stimulus,

i.e. sight of the ball, and the *start* of the movement.) Reaction time can be improved with practice to a certain extent. Batters will never be able to react at the same split second as the ball is seen to deviate quickly off the pitch.

Equally important is the ability to react and move ('response time'). It is little help in reacting quickly (in thought) to the ball moving off the pitch if you are slow moving to the ball! Given the strength and power training already outlined, the cricketer is advised to combine this with speed and agility drills.

Often the speed of response in the game can be improved through experience. This occurs because the player has become more efficient at 'reading' the game and can probably better anticipate what will happen next.

Assessing Speed and Agility

Assessing sprint speed is relatively easy to do, although the validity of such measures will depend on the accuracy of the timekeeper. Also, the distance used for sprint time-trials should be matched to the requirements of the players. For example, 40m sprint speed is often used as a measure of the type of speed needed in field team games like soccer. However, for cricket it may be relevant to assess players over 25m.

Agility is a feature prominent in cricket. A well-known test of agility is the Illinois Agility Run, shown in Fig 36.

FLEXIBILITY TRAINING

Flexibility – the most neglected area of sports fitness! Certainly this is the case for most sports with the possible exceptions of gymnastics, swimming and some athletics events. Most games players are notoriously inflexible. However, flexibility is important for several reasons:

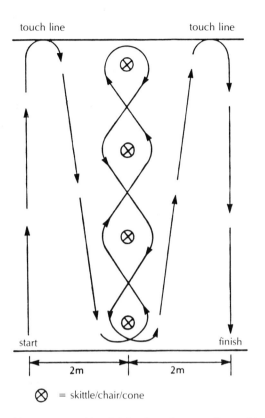

touch line   touch line

start   finish

|← 2m →|← 2m →|

⊗ = skittle/chair/cone

Note: start position is lying face down on floor with hands by the shoulders and head on the start line.

Fig 36   Illinois Agility Run, reproduced with permission from Adams, J. et al., Foundations of Physical Activity *(Stipes, 1965).*

(i)   Enhanced flexibility can help in the prevention and rehabilitation of injury.
(ii)   Poor flexibility can inhibit the development of some skills.
(iii) Poor flexibility can reduce the effectiveness of other fitness parameters.

To be sure, it is not just for dancers and gymnasts! Certainly serious cricketers need good flexibility and should be spending 5 to 10 minutes a day doing stretching exercises.

Methods of Flexibility Training

There are three main forms of flexibility training:

(i)   static flexibility
(ii)   ballistic flexibility
(iii) PNF (Proprioceptive neuromuscular facilitation!)

Static Flexibility

This method is when a muscle is stretched to the point of mild tension and then held for a length of time in the stretched position. This time can vary but it is recommended that it is not less than 10 seconds. Although some people suggest at least 30 seconds, this can be boring and likely to lead to players neglecting their flexibility training even though it could have a very beneficial physical effect.

Static stretching is a very effective form of flexibility and is recommended for all players. It should always be performed prior to vigorous activity and before ballistic flexibility exercises. The best time to improve flexibility is when the muscles are warm, so often a good time is after a game or training. However, static stretching should also be done prior to playing as part of the warm-up, as mentioned at the beginning of this chapter. The stretch continuum is shown in Fig 37. Players should

stop here

Preparatory Stretch	Developmental Stretch	Forceful Over-Stretch
as part of warm-up	to improve flexibility	too much
to prepare for activity	best done after vigorous exercise	not to be done

Fig 37   The stretch continuum.

Figure	Exercise	Muscles stretched	Starting position	Movement	Other points
43	Calf	Calf	Lean against wall, foot pointing forwards.	(i) To stretch outer calf, keep leg straight and push heel into groung. Push hips forwards; (ii) To stretch inner calf (soleus), bend leg and push forwards and downwards with hip. Keep heel on ground.	Vary position of toes.
44	Hamstring and lower back stretch	Hamstrings, lower back	Sit on floor, feet together and legs straight.	Sit up first (chest out), stretch forwards to the toes.	Vary leg positions (apart).
45	Hip stretch	Front of hip	Lunge position on floor.	Push hips forwards.	Progress to more upright trunk position with rear foot on toes.
46	Groin stretch	Groin, inside of thighs	Sit on floor, legs folded with soles of feet together.	Gently ease knees outwards and downwards.	Use pressure from arms if necessary.
47	Side stretch	Side (oblique) abdominals	Upright stance, feet astride.	Bend sideways and hold position.	Avoid leaning forwards.
48	Shoulder stretch	Shoulders, chest	(i) Standing. (ii) Seated – leg in front.	Lift arms upwards and backwards. Partner lifts arms upwards and backwards, or sideways.	(iii) If partner places a knee in the back of the exerciser, this can help stability.
49	Wrist stretch	Forearms	Kneeling on floor, hands flat.	Fingers pointing towards the body, pull shoulders back to stretch forearms.	Change direction of fingers.
50	Arm stretch	Shoulder, side of chest	Kneeling on all fours, arm outstretched.	Pull shoulder back to produce stretch on top of shoulder, arm and side of chest.	Reach out with hand first.
51	Lying stretch	(all-round stretch)	Lying face-up on floor.	Extend body position as much as possible.	

Fig 38   Explanations of static flexibility exercises.

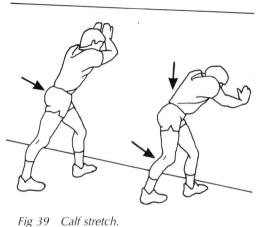

Fig 39   Calf stretch.

Fig 40   Hamstring and lower back stretch.

Fig 41   Hip stretch.

Fig 42   Groin stretch.

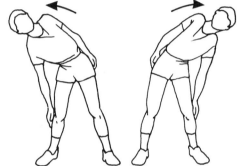

Fig 43   Side stretch.

Fig 44   Shoulder stretch.

Fig 45   Wrist stretch.

Fig 46   Arm stretch.

Fig 47   Lying stretch.

not stretch in a drastic way in the belief that 'more must be better'. Stretch to the point of mild tension, not pain!

Partners can be used to help stretch a little further, but remember that the athlete stretching should be in control. This is particularly important when groups of children are performing flexibility exercises.

Ballistic Flexibility

Ballistic stretching is where the muscles are stretched by using bouncing or 'bobbing' movements at the end of the range. There has been some controversy over this type of stretching as it has been indicated in the cause of some injuries. However, while it is never recommended for people on health-related exercise programmes (particularly older people or those with a history of joint injury), it is important for sports participants. This is because most sports require their participants to stretch while moving! Ballistic stretching, therefore, is required in sport, although precautions should be taken to avoid injury. This includes a good warm-up (including static stretches, to prepare the body for more ballistic activity. Care should be taken that at the end of the range of motion, where the movement is taking place, the bouncing/bobbing is controlled and gradual. These types of stretches should be specific to the movement required in cricket (e.g. forward arm circling for bowlers).

PNF Flexibility

PNF is a more advanced but highly effective method of stretching. It involves three stages:

(i)   Contraction of the muscle to be stretched (for about 10 seconds).
(ii)   Relaxation of the same muscle.
(iii)   Contraction of antagonist (opposite) muscle, or use partner assistance, to stretch the muscle.

The technique is thought to be effective due to the initial muscular contraction and its effect on the stretch receptors. This allows the muscle to be stretched further (see Alter, 1988, for more detail on PNF).

Most of the exercises shown can be adapted for PNF. However, remember that muscular contraction will not be effective without something to work against. Apparatus or partner resistance, therefore, is required. Use the static method when stretching during PNF. (See Figs 38 and 50 for explanations of the flexibility exercises; and see Alter, 1988, and Anderson, 1980; also Figs 39–49.)

Fig 48   PNF hamstring stretch.

Fig 49   PNF shoulder stretch.

Figure	Exercise	Muscles stretched	Starting position	Movement	Other points
52	PNF hamstring stretch	Hamstrings	Sitting on floor, feet together and legs straight.	Contraction: push against partner and push down into the ground with both legs (10 secs), then relax. Stretch: reach forwards (with or without partner assistance) towards toes.	
53	PNF shoulder stretch	Shoulder, chest	Sitting or kneeling, arms out-stretched to the side, parallel with floor.	Contraction: pull arms forwards against partner resistance (10 secs), then relax. Stretch: partner pulls arms back, keeping them parallel to the floor.	Can also be done with arms above head.

Fig 50   Explanations of PNF flexibility exercises.

Problem Flexibility Exercises

Not all flexibility exercises are necessarily good exercises. Because you are stretching muscles, you are also putting strain on joints. In most cases, the joints (as well as ligaments and tendons) are being stretched in an accept-able way. However, sometimes the joint can be twisted in such a way, or put under pressure, such that the exercise is potentially harmful. Two of the most common flexibility exercises which should, in most cases, be avoided are shown in Figs 51 and 52. The ballistic standing toe touch can lead to back problems. It should *never* be performed by people who have had back trouble in the past. It is better for all athletes to use the sit and reach exercise (Fig 54). Also, the hurdler stretch (Fig 52) can be a problem for those with knee injuries and should therefore be avoided by players who are at risk of injuring this part of the body (e.g.

Fig 51   Ballistic standing toe touch.

Devon Malcolm (England). A formidable prospect: the controlled power and flexibility of a fast bowler.

fast bowlers). Although this exercise can be effective in improving the flexibility of the hamstrings and groin, it puts a great deal of pressure on the knee joint.

Developing flexibility, like the other components of fitness, requires planning. The FITT principle, as it relates to flexibility training for cricket players, is summarised in Fig 53.

Fig 52   Hurdler stretch.

FITT component	Suggested guide-lines
Frequency	Can be done every day once some experience has been gained. Initially, every other day.
Intensity	To point of mild tension in the stretched muscle.
Time	Each exercise 10–30secs. Each session 5–15mins.
Type (of exercise)	Static stretches, followed by PNF and ballistic. Progress from preparatory to developmental stretching.

Fig 53   FITT principle for flexibility exercises.

Assessing Flexibility

Any of the flexibility exercises could be used as tests by simply recording measurements. However, two tests of flexibility are recommended here.

The first is the 'sit and reach' test (Fig 54) and is a good indication of flexibility in the hamstrings and the lower back. This is an important part of the body in which to have good flexibility as it can help prevent lower back problems.

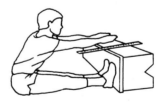

Fig 54   Sit and reach flexibility test.

The second test is the lying shoulder reach test (Fig 55). It is important for players bowling and fielding to have good shoulder flexibility.

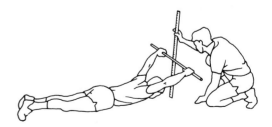

Fig 55   Lying shoulder reach test.

CHAPTER COOL-DOWN

After covering the main aspects of physical fitness for cricket, it is appropriate to cool-down before moving on to the next chapter! Our cool-down will be a summary of the main points:

(i)   Physical fitness for cricket is multi-dimensional, the main components requiring physical training are: cardio respiratory fitness (stamina), muscular endurance, strength and power, speed, and flexibility.

(ii)   Proper planning of fitness training must take into account the frequency, intensity, time and type of exercises (FITT principle), as well as specificity and reversibility.

(iii)   Cricketers should always warm up and cool down.

(iv)   Flexibility has often been a articularly neglected aspect of training but is an immensely important component of fitness.

3 Healthy Eating

Competitors must be well-prepared physically on the day of competition. This preparation involves many training sessions over the previous months or years. Food has been providing the energy for the body maintenance and general day-to-day activity as well as providing the energy needed to train. Other nutrients in the food – protein, vitamins and minerals – have been used to replete body losses incurred each day. Food is crucial for our health and well-being as well as allowing us to play cricket.

Food is also important to us on a psychological and social level. It may be psychologically important to eat favourite foods before a game as they are believed to help performance. These foods (often highly peculiar to an individual) may indeed ensure that peak performance is reached but it is unlikely to be because our bodies need the nutrients physiologically. However, if eating a certain food helps us to have that winning confidence then that's what matters. Sometimes, as we shall see later, there are certain foods which should be avoided on physiological grounds as they can damage performance.

On a social level, food gives us great pleasure. We all enjoy eating with a group of friends. Often the group will decide where to eat and this can be influenced by nearby restaurants or cafes and the price of food. Serious athletes may find themselves somewhere where the choice is limited and perhaps not quite suitable and anyway do not want to appear too different by choosing foods which are different from their friends. Players may, therefore, have to choose foods which they know are unsuitable. If this happens on an occasional basis it does not matter, but if it is a regular occurrence then it is important to ask the question, why?, and whether performance could be improved by eating foods which are more likely to be beneficial to performance.

Eating for your sport has two basic elements: eating for training (as this happens regularly and repeatedly then food choice must satisfy demands of training and also good general health) and eating for competition. Both are influenced by who we are, where we are and who we find ourselves with.

REQUIREMENTS FOR FOOD

Eating and drinking is taken for granted by most people. We eat and drink without too much thought and assume that our bodily needs will be met. Most of the time these needs will be met. But whether these needs are being met optimally is the significant question.

The human body is marvellously resilient, tolerant and versatile. If food-energy intake is less than the body needs, then the body simply conserves energy in order to 'balance the books'. People on reducing diets have been observed to be less active and physically slower than they were before embarking on their diet. This has implications for the person who is training and at the same time is deliberately reducing food intake. Can the same effort be put into training? Probably not. Young children when fed less than they need become less active and grow less quickly as the body attempts to balance its 'energy books'. If a young player is exercising hard and not able to eat a sufficient amount, then it is likely that either growth and/or the level of effort sustainable will suffer. It is not possible to get energy out if insufficient energy foods are consumed.

However, there comes a point when the body can no longer adapt to an insufficient level and at this point general body function begins to deteriorate very noticeably. Body tissues are not repaired efficiently (injury may take longer to heal) or there is weight loss, levels of activity become poor, and general health often deteriorates with increased prevalence to infection. Professional investigation and rectification may be essential at this point.

The body thus has an adaptive capability and a deficiency response. At the other end of the spectrum (and by far the most likely to occur in the West) it reacts to excessive energy intake. Food intake above requirement will not raise the level of activity or turn individuals into super-performers, although it will encourage rapid growth: in children upwards, and in adults – outwards! Eating more protein than the body needs or can use, simply results in the excess being (expensively!) excreted. The same is true of water-soluble vitamins such as vitamin C and some minerals such as sodium (salt). In the case of fat-soluble vitamins such as vitamin A, and certain minerals such as iron which the body cannot so easily dispose of, excess stores can ultimately be life-threatening. Athletes, therefore, need to take special care with regard to the dangers of over-indulgence, especially when it comes to diet supplements. Regular monitoring of body weight can provide information about meeting nutrient requirements or meeting them in excess! A useful guide is the Government publication, *Recommended Amounts of Food Energy and Nutrients for Groups of People in the UK* (DHSS, 1979).

There is no evidence that sportspeople need any more food than non-sporting individuals, provided that they are eating a good variety of foods which will meet their energy needs.

Merv Hughes (Australia) bowling an inswinger or an outswinger? A good batter might spot the difference even before the ball is released.

These needs may well vary from season to season and during different training periods. The total amount of food, as well as the types of food consumed, may also vary.

In summary, the overall needs of the athlete in training will be unique and variable. This variation may be masked by the ability of the individual to adapt to different levels of nutrition. It is essential that such adaptation is not allowed to mask impending deficiency. Sportspeople and their coaches must remain vigilant.

WHAT IS IN FOOD?

Food is a mixture of nutrients – fat, carbohydrate, protein, vitamins and minerals. These basic constituents are assembled into cells which enable plants or animals to live and grow.

Everyone needs these nutrients in the same way. Eating food enables these nutrients to be available for our own body cells and functions. All naturally-occurring foods contain all nutrients but they are present in differing amounts (dependent on the actual function which that food had on the plant or in the animal). For example, leaves are not storage organs and so their energy content is low. Meat on the other hand is muscle and so has a high protein content.

A list of foods and some of the nutrients they contain is shown in Fig 56. The carbohydrate and fat foods provide the most energy in our diets but you will see that they also can provide protein, vitamins and minerals. The lists are put together in a way which allows you to choose amounts of food which provide similar amounts of carbohydrate (CHO), fat and protein. A more comprehensive list is given in the Government publication *Manual of Nutrition* (HMSO, 1985).

As foods are mixtures of nutrients it is difficult to say one food is better than another. For example, if we said that cheese was bad because of its fat content and omitted it from the diet then you would also omit an important source of protein and calcium. Therefore it is wise to eat from a wide variety of foods then there will not be excessive amounts of any one nutrient. Eating plenty of fruit and vegetables which are low in fat will help to balance those foods which contain relatively high amounts of fat.

Sources of Carbohydrate

Milk and milk products – also provide significant amounts of calcium.

1 glass of milk	Supplies about 8g protein, 12g CHO, 8g fat, 150kcals.
For reduced energy and fat: 1 glass of skimmed milk 1 carton plain yoghurt	Each portion supplies about 8g protein, 12g CHO, 80kcals.

Cereals and legumes – high carbohydrate and some protein*.
1 thin/medium slice bread (white*)
½ roll, bun, breadcake, crumpet, teacake.
1 tbs flour (white)*
1 digestive biscuit
  (add 1 'fat' portion)
4tbs unsweetened breakfast cereal*
3tbs baked beans or other cooked
  bean*/pea*/lentil*
  (add ⅓ 'meat' portion)
3–4tbs fresh/processed peas cooked
1tbs apple crumble/pie
  (add 1 'fat' portion and 1 'fruit'
  portion)

Each portion supplies about 2g protein, 15g CHO as starch and 70kcals.

Fruit and vegetables – also supply important vitamins.
Small apple, pear, orange
½ small banana
10–12 cherries or grapes
2 medium (or equivalent dried) plums,
  prunes, apricots, dates
1tbs raisins, currants
2tbs any vegetable except avocado –
  (add 4 'fat' portions)
1 small/medium potato (boiled or baked)
  (if fried add 1 'fat' portion *see* below)

Each portion supplies about 0–2g protein, 5–10g CHO as sugars and 25–40kcals.

Sources of Fat
Small scrap butter or margarine (5g)
1tsp oil
2tsp mayonnaise Each portion supplies about
1 slice fried streaky bacon 5g fat, 45kcals.
5 olives
10 roasted peanuts
2tsp double cream

Sources of Protein
Meat and fish – also rich sources of
  minerals*.
2–3oz cooked (not fried) meat* or
  fatty/oily fish Each portion supplies about
2oz hard cheese 20–25g protein, 15–20g fat,
3oz edam/gouda/brie-type cheese 200–250kcals.
3 grilled sausages (add 1 'fat' portion)

For reduced energy and fat:
2–3oz cooked chicken (no skin),
  veal or rabbit Each portion supplies about
2–3oz cooked liver* 20–25g protein, 5g fat,
2–3oz white fish 150kcals, but do not fry or
2–3oz of tuna in brine or 4 pilchards add fat (unless from portion).
6oz cottage cheese

*Fig 56   Nutrients contained in typical portions of food. This list is not
exhaustive. If you want to learn more, consult a food composition table
(see Further Reading). Also, remember that certain foods may make
contributions not only to the group they are in, but also to others. For
example, a piece of apple pie makes a contribution to the carbohydrate, fat, protein
and mineral content of the diet.*

Sources of Thiamin or Vitamin B1
Milk and milk products All milk and soya milk
Cereals and legumes All legumes** and fortified (non-
  wholemeal) bread** and flour
  products and fortified
  breakfast cereals
Meat and fish Ham and pork products, liver
Fruit and vegetables None
Other Brewers' yeast

Sources of Riboflavin or Vitamin B2
Milk and milk products All types of milk**
Cereals and legumes Only fortified breakfast cereals

Meat and fish	Liver
Fruit and vegetables	Dark-green leafed vegetables
Other	Brewers' yeast

Sources of Pyridoxine or Vitamin B6

Milk and milk products	None
Cereals and legumes	All legumes**
Meat and fish	Beef, pork, lamb, tuna and salmon
Fruit and vegetables	Bananas and potatoes
Other	Nuts

Sources of Calcium

Milk and milk products	All milk**, (cheese*), yoghurt
Cereals and legumes	Fortified flour and products (non-wholemeal), tofu
Meat and fish	Salmon and sardines if bones consumed
Fruit and vegetables	Dark-green leafed vegetables
Other	Molasses and unhulled sesame seeds as in tahini

Sources of Iron

Milk and milk products	None
Cereals and legumes	Fortified flour and products**, fortified breakfast cereals, all legumes**
Meat and fish	Red meats**, liver**
Fruit and vegetables	Dark-green leafed vegetables
Other	Molasses, chocolate and cocoa

Sources of Zinc

Milk and milk products	Cheese
Cereals and legumes	All legumes, bread, wholemeal flour and products
Meat and fish	Meat**, liver, crab and shellfish
Fruit and vegetables	Very small amounts
Other	Nuts

* also rich in iron
** particularly rich source

Fig 57 Sources of vitamins and minerals.

THE NEED FOR FLUID, NUTRIENTS AND ENERGY.

Fluid

Our bodies are about 70 per cent water: i.e. in a 70kg person, 49kg is water. Cells and blood need water in order to dissolve and carry nutrients. Water is also needed to cool the body – very important during exercise. Even a slight reduction in body water content (2 to 5 per cent or 1.5 to 3.5 litres) can cause a reduced efficiency in cellular function. People are observed to lose their power of concentration and perform poorly overall. Dehydration allows the body insufficient water to cool itself and the body can overheat. Fluid or water must be replaced. Fluid balance or hydration must therefore be of prime importance to all sportspeople. Water is normally lost in three ways:

(i)   Through the urine. This volume can be increased by consuming certain nutrients such as alcohol (known as the diuretic effect).

(ii)   Through the skin. This normally accounts for a small percentage loss, but during exercise can rise to over 3 litres per hour depending on the intensity of exercise and the environmental conditions (high humidity inhibits loss and we therefore feel hotter).

(iii)   Through the lungs.

Water can also be lost abnormally in two ways:

(i)   Through diarrhoea. This may be caused by infection or by eating too much fibre or large amounts of simple carbohydrate. Both cannot be absorbed and therefore cause water to be drawn into the gut from the body tissues (causing cell dehydration).

(ii)   Through fevers. Extra water is lost through the skin to try and reduce body temperature.

Clearly, avoiding extra fluid loss is important. Avoiding food and drink which may be contaminated (even ice cubes made from impure water can cause infection) means being cautious about using foods from dubious origins. It is also important to know how much of other foods can be tolerated by your system, e.g. dried fruits which are both high in fibre and simple carbohydrates. The amount which is tolerated can also be dependent on circumstances. For example, there are some poeple who, when apprehensive, tend to have loose bowel movements thus increasing water loss.

Replacing the fluid lost during training and competition is vital. Our normal thirst mechanisms often do not detect large losses (e.g. during training sessions) and we may therefore fail to make good the fluid needed. Water losses need to be monitored actively, even if this means weighing yourself before and after any exercise. The change in weight will reflect the change in body water content and hence the amount that needs replacing. This must be replaced. The best way to do this is to use a drink which is isotonic to body fluids (the same concentration) or hypotonic (weaker concentration). But the drink should *never* be hypertonic (more concentrated) because body fluid will be drawn into the gut to dilute it. This causes (osmotic) diarrhoea and is counterproductive. It has been found that a solution of:

> 2.5g of sugar per 100ml
> 1.0mmol of sodium (23mg) per 100ml
> 0.5mmol of potassium (20mg) per 100ml

served cold (as from the fridge) in about 0.25 litre quantities is ideal. Fortunately a dilute solution of orange squash, say 2 tablespoons per litre, is just about the correct concentration.

If using a commercially prepared drink it is wise to check the concentration. It should not be greater than those given above. Plain water is also acceptable. Whatever is chosen it is important to consume an amount to replace that lost.

It takes some practice and training to consume the amount lost during training sessions. Cricket players need to be very vigilant especially if working hard in hot conditions.

A drink which contains alcohol, as we have seen, causes extra urinary loss of water – it is a diuretic. Therefore, pints of beer will not do! Caffeine also has diuretic properties.

Finally, before competition it is helpful for individuals to prepare for the fluid which is to be lost. If you have carefully monitored losses during training and competitions you can predict how much you will lose. If you consume some fluid before the match to cover anticipated losses this can help you to maintain concentration and activity levels.

Nutrients

The overall food and nutritional requirements of each athlete will depend on: age, sex and body-weight (growing children/teenagers need proportionally greater amounts of food than adults; women need more iron than men; men need more energy because they often weigh more) and on duration and intensity of exercise undertaken.

It is interesting that the amount of energy needed is the most variable and depends on the factors outlined above. The need for protein, minerals and vitamins is less variable.

ENERGY

Energy is derived from fat and carbohydrate in food and, to a lesser extent, protein. The amount of energy in the food is measured in units corresponding to the amount of heat that food will produce when it is 'burned' in the body.

The heat thus produced can be thought of as providing the power to make the body work in much the same way as a coal fire produces heat to make steam to turn an engine. The units of heat are calories. A calorie is a very tiny amount of heat and the amount in food is thousands of calories or kilocalories (kcals).

Another unit which is used to measure the amount of energy in food is the joule, again, a very tiny unit of work-energy and so it is expressed in kilojoules (kJ). One kilocalorie is equivalent to 4.2 kilojoules (1kcal = 4.2kJ). Large amounts of kilojoules are expressed as megajoules (MJ), that is 1,000kJ to a megajoule.

Energy in the food is used to do internal work in our bodies, keeping the heart beating and the lungs and other organs working, even when we are asleep. This requirement for energy is known as the Basal Metabolic Rate (BMR) and varies with body size. The BMR has priority over all dietary energy supply.

The other basic need for energy is in the renewal of body tissues and the excretion of waste products. Renewal of our body tissue takes place all the time but sometimes when exercising very hard new muscle tissue is made. You may do this during training sessions to strengthen arm or leg muscles. The amount of energy required to make about a pound of muscle tissue is thought to be about 5,000 to 7,000kcals.

After the energy needs for keeping the body 'ticking over' have been met the rest of the energy supply can be put towards doing 'external' work or exercise. The amount of external work or exercise which can be undertaken can therefore be highly dependent upon just how much energy is left from the amount initially available. In some cases where demands for exercise are allowed to override energy needs for basic maintenance or growth, then individuals become thin, undernourished and underdeveloped.

CARBOHYDRATES

Plants store their energy as carbohydrate (CHO). This is a term used to cover a variety of molecules which all have similar chemical properties.

Some molecules are small and taste sweet and are known as simple, or sugary, carbohydrate. They include glucose, sucrose (sugar), fructose, maltose and lactose. (Lactose is an anomaly as it is produced by animals for milk for their young.)

Some molecules are large, do not taste sweet and are known as complex, or starchy, carbohydrate. The starches in bread, potatoes, rice and pasta (macaroni/spaghetti) are all starchy or complex.

Finally, there are some forms of carbohydrate which we cannot digest or absorb and which are known as unavailable carbohydrate, or dietary fibre. Eventually *all* dietary sources of the sugary and starchy carbohydrate, sometimes collectively called available CHO, will be transformed into glucose and carried to the cells by the blood.

Each gram of available CHO (from starch and sugars) provides 4kcals of energy to the body. It is found in all foods of plant origin: cereals, fruit, vegetables (including pulses; dried peas, beans and lentils) and to a limited extent in nuts (see Fig 56).

Fruit and vegetables contain a very high percentage of water and the carbohydrate which is present is much diluted. For this reason these foods are less energy dense (this also applies to other nutrients which are similarly 'diluted'). It also means that to consume a large amount of energy a great quantity of these foods needs to be eaten. This is useful for slimmers, but not necessarily for the person who requires a high-energy intake in a hurry.

However, the foods made from cereal grains, bread, pasta and biscuits/cakes do not have as much water content and are more dense with respect to carbohydrate and energy. Bread, breakfast cereals, pasta and rice are all rich sources of CHO and are relatively energy dense.

Once the CHO is consumed it appears in the blood as glucose. This can be used directly for energy or it can be stored in the muscle/liver as glycogen, the animal equivalent of starch. This is a very important source of energy to animal cells. There is a finite amount of glycogen which can be stored, about 200g. The glycogen in the muscle probably determines the amount of work which can be done by the muscle. Any excess glucose is then made into fat and stored in the adipose tissue.

FATS

Fat is found in almost all foods as it is an important part of the cell walls found in all plants and animals. Plants do not store energy as fat, except in nuts, so the amount of fat in plant sources of food will be very tiny. Animals, including humans, store energy in their bodies as fat. An average woman may have 10kg of fat stored. Such fat is stored in many places: in adipose tissue around vital organs, under the skin and amongst muscle fibres. Therefore, meat or animal products, eggs, milk products and milk itself all contain fat, often in significant amounts (*see* Fig 56).

Fat is energy dense. It supplies 9kcals per gram, twice as much per unit weight as CHO. Animal products do not contain as much water as fruit and vegetables and are therefore more energy (and nutrient) dense. Fat also tastes nice (think of the taste of fried mushrooms compared to boiled, or butter on toast rather than dry toast). Eating fat is easy and because it is energy dense it provides energy in small amounts of food. It is easy to overindulge. The slimmer needs to beware as does the cricketer who does not want to go on the field with an extra tyre!

DIET AND LONG-TERM HEALTH

The amount and type of food energy we consume may influence our health. It is generally

Chris Broad on the way to another century through skill and stamina of mind and body, sustained by a healthy diet.

agreed that there is a weight for height ratio at which adults are fitter and less prone to develop various life-threatening diseases. The more fat you have 'on board' the higher will be the ratio.

A simple way to determine whether your weight to height ratio is satisfactory is to use this internationally accepted calculation: weight (kg) divided by height (metres) squared. This is termed the Body Mass Index (BMI). The range thought to be acceptable is 17 to 25. If it is below the bottom end this is just as disturbing as if it is too high. Lean people *may* be more agile and active but if weight is reduced too far then it indicates poor body reserves of nutrients because of a restrictive dietary intake. A very restrictive intake can lead to nutrient deficiencies which will ultimately affect performance.

BMI is, then, a simple and quick test but it does not tell us how much of an individual is fat, and how much is lean (muscle), tissue. To find out the ratio of fat to lean a more specific measurement has to be made. A method which can be used is based on the assumption that the fat under the skin is a fair reflection of total body fat. Using special, skinfold callipers (*see* Fig 58), the amount of fat under the skin can be measured. The total body fat can then be estimated by using an equation (Eisenman and Johnson, 1982). Women, for physiological reasons, always have a higher percentage of body fat than men. The amount of fat which different people have varies and can be manipulated by use of exercise and diet. However, the difference between men and women always remains. A list of measured body fats is given below:

Average adult male (20–50 years)
    15–25 per cent fat
Average adult female (20–50 years)
    26–35 per cent fat

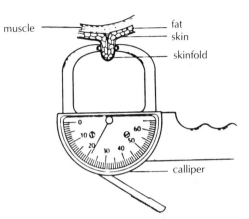

Fig 58   Estimating body fat with skinfold callipers.

Adult male tennis player
    about 16 per cent fat
Adult female tennis player
    about 20 per cent fat

Adult male runner (distance)
    6–13 per cent fat
Adult female runner (distance)
    15–19 per cent fat

A cricketer would probably wish to have the same body fat as an average adult.

PROTEIN

The requirement for dietary protein depends on several factors:

(i)   The amount of muscle tissue present: the more muscle tissue, the more body protein there is to maintain and replace.
(ii)   The amount of new tissue synthesis (in the growth phase proportionally more protein is required plus the energy to synthesise it).
(iii)   The fractions of protein lost through sweat and hair/skin loss.

99

Much controversy surrounds the nature of the body's need for protein. The body can become very efficient at conserving its store of protein which is found in all cells in the body. It would seem that sportspeople need the same amount of protein per kilogram of body weight as do untrained individuals. But this is strongly influenced by the energy supply of the diet. If there is insufficient energy in the diet then either food protein *or* body protein can be used as a source of energy. This is very wasteful because once it is used for energy it cannot be used for body protein repair.

The amount of protein required is therefore closely related to how well energy supply meets demand. If enough carbohydrate and fat are consumed to supply energy then sportspeople need no more protein than anyone else. But some people may take supplementary protein. Unfortunately this form of protein, unlike in normal foods, does not have fat or carbohydrate with it. Therefore the energy supply may be less than needed and the protein can be wasted. Work currently in progress at Leeds Polytechnic (unpublished) tends to indicate that the consumption of protein supplements can actually cause some athletes to reduce their overall food intake. This is clearly counter-productive in terms of maintaining an adequate energy and nutrient supply.

Finally, protein will *only* be used to build new tissue if there is an appropriate training programme. Of course you need plenty of energy to maintain training so the argument once again revolves around the need for, and high priority of, energy foods in the diet.

Amino acids are the tiny molecules which are joined together in unique sequences to make proteins. Proteins in hair will have a different sequence to the proteins in muscle which is why hair doesn't look the same as muscle! Once again, all proteins contain all amino acids but in different amounts, depending on source and function. Generally, proteins from animal sources are nearer in amino acid pattern and proportion to our own bodies and

our needs. However, it is possible to get all these amino acids from plant sources. Vegetarians do this and are perfectly healthy. So it is possible to get all the amino acids and protein from the cheaper vegetable sources of protein, such as baked beans. By mixing foods together a better mix of amino acids is ensured. Putting cereals (bread, pasta, rice) together with nuts or pulses (dried beans, peas or lentils) creates a perfect complement of amino acids precisely the same as that found in the best sirloin.

How Much Protein?

The actual amount one needs is difficult to say. It is possible to give values for grams of protein, but this is meaningless unless it is put into the context of food. Values for adults of between 1g to 2g protein/kg of body weight/day have been given. For someone who weighs 80kg the need for protein could be estimated at 80g to 160g/day. (The values quoted in the DHSS recommended intake tables are comparable to this.) About 40kcals of energy are required per gram of protein. In the above example this would mean a food energy intake of between 3,200 and 6,400kcals per day.

But food is a mixture of nutrients and if the food in the diet provides say 3,000kcals, then this amount is likely to contain at least 80g of protein or probably a lot more. It is very difficult to consume too little protein when eating a variety of foods. (For some sources of protein in foods, *see* Fig 56.)

VITAMINS AND MINERALS

There is also little evidence to suggest that athletes have a greater bodily demand for vitamins compared to non-athletes. Food is a mixture of nutrients and as food intake rises (as it must do to support activity) then so does the level of vitamin supply through the food.

A very bizarre diet indeed would have to be chosen for any deficiency to occur. However, it is possible to overindulge in vitamin supplements and this can be dangerous. It is becoming apparent that not only can over-indulging in vitamins (even vitamin C) lead to the development of harmful conditions, but also that such supplementation affects the absorption of other nutrients. Individuals should take care and, if supplementation is thought necessary, they should seek medical advice to confirm a positive need.

Minerals may be thought of in two groups, those which we require in relatively large amounts and those which we require in trace amounts. The former, which are of importance here, are sodium, potassium and calcium. Of those required in very small amounts the most important is iron.

Sodium and potassium loss in sweat barely reach levels whereby supplementation is required above normal dietary intake and therefore they should not be considered outside the context of a normal varied diet. But there is perhaps slightly more concern over adequate iron intake in athletes due to the occasional occurrence of the condition known as 'sports anaemia' although it has not been described in cricketers.

The reason for this anaemia is not fully understood and may result from physical stress on the red blood cells or from abnormal losses of blood both due to the intensity and prolonged effort of training and exercise. If anaemia is diagnosed then iron supplementation will be advised. Also it would be wise to make sure the diet contains iron-rich foods (see Fig 57).

A more serious cause of concern are those sportspeople (and it usually is the female) who deliberately restrict food intake to slim. When food is restricted then the supply of nutrients is reduced overall. This is especially critical with respect to iron and calcium both of which are crucial to health in the long and short term. Women who exercise hard and who limit their diet compensate for inadequate dietary supplies of iron by ceasing to menstruate. This is an indication that hormonal changes have occurred which are not normal.

The other system which these changes affect is the synthesis and resynthesis of bone. On a low calcium intake (poor dietary supply) where some hormonal levels are low, bone is not effectively calcified and a condition known as osteoporosis occurs. Any exercise which is isometric in nature (i.e. puts a strain on the long bones) helps to counteract this process to an extent, but the disturbing feature is that it is not known how the damage will manifest itself once serious sport is stopped. Women in particular should pay attention to their overall food, calcium and iron intake. Again, if the food energy in a varied diet is in excess of 2,000kcals there should be no problem in meeting the needs for iron and calcium. Fig 57 also shows sources of calcium and other vitamins in the diet.

Overall, the athlete who is not restricting intake should not need any supplementation of vitamins or minerals. In any event supplementation should only be commenced when a deficiency is suspected and then confirmed.

TRAINING SCHEDULES AND FOOD FOR COMPETITIONS

Rest periods are critical to successful training in order to allow the individual to replenish energy and nutrient stores (i.e. simply to eat). A schedule needs to be established to allow time to be available for the preparation (including shopping) and eating of food. Without food we simply do not have the energy available to perform. It is therefore an essential part of the training schedule. It may well be that rest days or relaxation of the training schedule become eating periods, although this should not mean that these days become ones of over indulgence.

Timing of meals should be such that the

major part of digestion is complete before activity commences. Fat and protein foods, on the whole, take longer to move through the stomach and small intestine: about 2 to 4 hours. Carbohydrate and cold foods are much quicker: about 1 to 2 hours depending on the size of the meal. Sportspeople need to eat after a training session and good anticipation of food needs is essential. As it may not be possible to buy or have time to eat an appropriate meal, it is better to take some sandwiches and a flask of fluid to provide the essential nutrient and fluid replacement. If you do have to eat out then baked potatoes and/or pizza/pasta make the most sensible snacks or meals. Meals and snacks should always be based around the starchy carbohydrates, as they are more effective at repleting glycogen stores lost during competition or during training.

TRAINING FOR CRICKET

Training for cricket, which is largely a sport performed under aerobic conditions, is primarily to enhance the cardiovascular system and muscle. This ensures efficient and continuous supply of fuel and oxygen to the muscles over a long period. Training sessions at sub-maximal work load (i.e. aerobic) also condition the body to use its fat stores as the major fuel.

Aerobic conditioning means long training sessions which are also expensive in terms of energy usage. Time to take food on board is therefore of the essence. Concentrated sources of CHO are important (see Fig 56). High energy foods (i.e. containing fat) such as chocolate, rich cakes, nuts and biscuits should be consumed with care as they can cause fat gain. It is essential that all lost fluids are replaced.

Athletes in cricket may also need to think critically about their lean to fat ratio as carrying too much fat can impede mobility. Consideration of excess body fat is an important part of

training but it is vital that the level of body fat achieved is easily maintained. Constant dieting does little to afford the energy for effective training.

Reducing body fat should therefore be done slowly so as not to impede the ability to train and perform. Reducing the amount consumed in general and especially the fat containing foods is appropriate. The amount of alcohol consumed should also be monitored and reduced. Loss of body fat should proceed at about 0.5kg per week. New eating habits should be formed to maintain this new weight.

COMPETITION

As competition time approaches then the suggested training programme must be combined with the psychological will to win. Food can have a role to play in the latter, but food eaten immediately before competition has little effect on subsequent performance; it can in fact be detrimental. It is the extended period of preparation, including training and diet which will affect performance 'on the day'. Fluid and hydration 'on the day', however, unlike food, are major elements in success.

How to Arrive with a Full Tank

The message of this chapter is to ensure that one gets the 'energy books balanced' – and that means ensuring energy is replaced in the working muscle.

The spacing and planning of meals and snacks before or during a match is very important. As already mentioned, it is important to have the intestine as free as possible from the process of digestion. Meals should therefore be finished at least two hours before playing (and preferably four hours), as the anticipation of a match may actually reduce intestinal function. Individuals should carefully plan those meals which they *feel* will be most beneficial 'on the day' – remember the psychological value of foods.

The content of the meals is largely irrelevant in terms of providing energy (this has already been stored). Sugary snacks should be avoided as these may delay the release of internal energy and make you feel sluggish. It is also wise to avoid those foods which are known to produce flatulence. If something sugary is taken about 45 minutes before starting a match then the body will be 'caught out' and will not react as well to exercise. The body will be expecting to store food/nutrients and not to mobilise fuel. The hormones which act to control body chemistry will not promote energy release and this can be very unfortunate for the athlete!

However, if something sugary is taken once the match is started then this glucose is used by the muscles. Though you cannot stop in the middle of a match to take a sugary drink or food, it should be remembered that during rest periods you can replace some of the glucose which has inevitably been used by your muscles during play.

Players may be tempted to take ergogenic aids such as caffeine but caffeine is a drug. If it is given in large and medically uncontrolled amounts it can produce vascular changes which can be harmful. In addition, everyday doses of caffeine can have a pronounced diuretic effect which is not particularly desirable when hydration is required.

Hydration is probably the single most important factor to success on the day. It is essential that fluid is replaced as often as possible throughout the match. The concept of fluid with a suitable concentration to ensure maximum absorption has been discussed already, but it may help to supplement it with some sugar and glucose during play.

Eating between matches should follow the same basic rules and be completed at least two hours before the next competition. Some digestion and absorption of food does occur at submaximal levels of exercise. Each individual should note what types of food can be easily consumed between matches and which to avoid.

SUMMARY

Eating for serious cricket players should be taken just as seriously as their training schedule and should be part of it. Food provides the fuel for play and the nutrients to keep the body healthy. To ignore these basic facts is to jeopardise success at your sport. Limiting food or not planning meals can be counterproductive. Monitoring of both food intake and body weight should be a fundamental part of your routine.

4 Injury Prevention

CLASSIFICATION OF INJURY

In order to prevent injuries it is preferable to understand why and where they occur in the body. An injury may be due to an external force (extrinsic injury) or to a force within the body (intrinsic injury). A cricket ball hitting a player on the head, two players colliding with each other or a player falling on the ground awkwardly would be classified as extrinsic injuries. Intrinsic injuries may happen without any particular cause (incidental injury) but they are more likely to occur when the training load is rapidly increased in intensity and frequency (overuse injury).

Most injuries tend to occur quite suddenly (acute injury) but fortunately tend to settle very quickly. However, an acute injury may progress and become a chronic injury which is usually more difficult to treat and takes longer to overcome. You are far more likely to get injured towards the end of a practice session or a match when you become tired than at any other time, so take more care as you become fatigued.

SITE OF INJURY

Sports injuries can occur anywhere in the body such as in muscles, tendons (pullies attached to the bone from muscles), tenosynovia (the protective sheaths around a tendon), ligaments (fibrous bands joining two bones together at a joint), joints and bones. It is helpful to grade the injuries into three groups:

Group A

Minimal damage when bruising only occurs and there is no major disruption to the muscle, tendon or ligament, etc. Small blood vessels are damaged, however, and leak blood which forms a bruise (haematoma).

Group B

Some disruption of the tissues takes place and a sprain, strain, partial tear or partial rupture takes place in a muscle, tendon (tendonitis), tendon sheath (tenosynovitis), ligament or bone (stress fracture).

Stress fractures of bones can be likened to the cracks in a piece of wire which has been repeatedly bent – at first the wire looks strong but eventually, if stressed enough it can break right through.

Group C

Complete ruptures of muscles, tendons, and ligaments, fractured or broken bones and dislocated joints.

AVOIDANCE OF INJURIES

The basic rule for avoiding injury is to increase your own fitness through increased speed, strength, endurance and flexibility. Using a training programme in a sensible, progressive

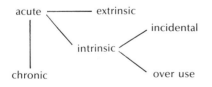

Fig 59 Classification of injury.

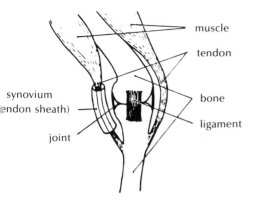

muscle

tendon

synovium
(tendon sheath)

bone

ligament

joint

Fig 60 Physiological representation of the knee.

way reduces the chances of sustaining intrinsic and overuse injuries. Skill plays not only an important part in achieving a better all-round player but also enables the player to avoid injury through inappropriate technique. While it is usual to practise your batting skills and bowling techniques it is equally important to practise all the skills needed as a fielder whether close to the wicket or in the outfield. Not only will it help with your game but it will reduce the chance of injury through faulty technique.

Warm-Up and Warm-Down

Warm-up is essential not only in preparation for matches but also in training. By gradually increasing the intensity of work and building up the number of skills to be rehearsed the body and mind are both being warmed up. The muscles are controlled by electrical impulses fed to them from the brain and this system needs tuning and adjusting just as the muscles need warming up. Equally as important is the warm-down, or unwind, when more emphasis is put on flexibility to test for minor injury that may have occurred during exercise. Gentle rhythmic movement helps in flushing out the waste products of metabolism from the muscles that build up during high-intensity exercise. Muscle stiffness the following day,

especially after a lengthy innings at the crease or a prolonged spell of bowling, can be reduced by performing a regular post-match or post-training drill of stretching and low-intensity exercise.

Protection

Most extrinsic injuries can be avoided by taking sensible precautions and checking the safety of the training venue and any equipment that is used in it. The gyms and indoor nets should be well ventilated and well lit, with any sharp edges, radiators or walls padded with foam. Doors and windows should be secured and other recreational equipment stored correctly and well out of the way of the training area. The netting, post and the ropes securing them must be checked to ensure that balls when hit hard do not go through. The pitch and outfield must be checked before each match or training session especially at the beginning of the season to make sure no sharp stones, glass or metal objects have been left on the grass. Sightscreens need cleaning at the beginning of the season and checked to see that they are secure or can be moved if appropriate. Weight-training equipment should only be used under supervision, check the thumb screws on free weights and see that the pins are correctly set on multigyms.

A few years ago the wearing of a protective helmet whether by the batsman facing a fast bowler or by a fielder close in was thought not to be cricket. Fortunately we live in a more enlightened world now and players should be encouraged to wear a well-fitting helmet in addition to pads that are light and comfortable to wear. If your batting gloves become worn out buy a new pair and use protective padding on the thigh and forearm if you do not feel safe facing a fast bowler on a hard pitch.

The clothing you wear should be well fitting, not so tight that it rubs causing abrasions nor too loose so that it gets in the way of free movement. Tops should be long-sleeved to prevent friction burns when playing on indoor or artificial surfaces. Shin guards worn by close fielders will reduce not only the number of sore legs but also cut down on some of the broken legs by reducing the force of impact.

Boots should be well fitting (wear new boots for short periods in training only until they feel comfortable, in order to cut down on blisters). Make sure you choose the right footwear for the right surface, you may need to have a different pair for damp and dry grass, for artificial surfaces and for wooden floors in gymnasiums.

Always remove dentures and on no account chew gum either training or playing in case you choke on it when injured. If you need to wear glasses check with your optician that the lenses and frames are shatterproof. Alternately wear soft contact lenses but try them out for some time in training before using them in a match.

Some players may wish to strap their fingers, ankles or feet, particularly if they have been injured in the past. The strapping needs to be inelastic, such as zinc oxide, in order to support joints adequately and must be removed after exercise allowing a full range of movement to take place. A trained physiotherapist can show you how to apply the tape.

Control

The rules of the game and the regulations controlling the use of training venues have been devised not only to ensure fair play but also to prevent injury. It is therefore prudent to observe these rules for your own safety. Children should play with and against people of your own physique and standard of play.

Self-control plays an important role in preventing and reducing injury. Try and organise your day so that adequate time is allowed for meals with at least two hours elapsing before training after a large meal. Most athletes need a minimum of eight hours sleep each night and time must also be allocated for training,

eating, studying or working. Fatigue will set in if not enough time is allowed for adequate rest between training sessions and fatigue is the biggest cause of most sports injuries.

Regular showering or bathing after training and frequent washing of kit will help reduce the incidence of fungal infections of the skin. Don't borrow other peoples' clothing or towels, make sure you always have clean, dry clothing to change into after a training session. Athletes should not smoke, not only for obvious health reasons but also because the nicotine in cigarettes attaches itself to the oxygen-carrying component of the red blood cells (haemoglobin) reducing the available space for oxygen to be transported to the muscles. This effect lasts for up to three weeks after the last cigarette has been smoked.

By tradition many cricketers drink alcohol not only after but sometimes during and before a match. Alcohol should never be consumed before a match or training session not only to avoid errors of judgement but also because alcohol will dehydrate the body and make the body less efficient. After a hard match or training session, particularly in hot conditions plain fluid should be drunk first before racing to the bar!

Check-List for Injury Prevention

(i) Environment: clothes; spectacles; boots; pads; helmets; shin guards; surfaces; equipment.

(ii) Control: training match/rules; physique.

(iii) Fitness: skill; strength; speed; endurance; flexibility.

(iv) Self-discipline: warm-up; diet; sleep; smoking; hygiene; alcohol.

MEDICAL PROBLEMS

Frequently it may be illness, not injury, that prevents the sportsman or woman from training. Any cricketer who has an infection, such as a heavy cold, a chest infection or 'flu, should not train or play, especially if the body temperature is elevated above normal (37°C) or if the resting pulse rate is appreciably higher than normal.

You won't be able to perform well and certainly won't get any beneficial training effect if you continue to train at this stage. You also run the risk of the infection getting worse and the heart muscle being affected (myocarditis).

Rest is a must until the illness passes. Low-grade chronic infections (e.g. of the teeth, skin or sinuses) may prevent you performing at peak level and treatment should be sought earlier rather than later. Some virus infections such as glandular fever may linger on for weeks; regrettably, there is no treatment and you must remain patient until the illness passes. Only then can you make a gradual return to full training.

Tetanus, or lockjaw, is an uncommon but severe illness which can be picked up from the soil through cuts and abrasions and is easily avoided by having a vaccination against it. You should have a booster injection for tetanus at least every ten years.

Dehydration

A reduction in body weight of 1 per cent by lost sweat results in a 10 per cent reduction in work capacity. It is therefore vital that any sweat lost is adequately and promptly replaced by water, not only to enhance performance, but also to prevent injury. Some people particularly when training regularly may become chronically dehydrated with a subsequent reduction in body weight, reduced urine output and a rise in resting pulse. Take every opportunity to drink fluids during a long day in the field or during a long innings at the crease. Thirst alone is not a reliable indication of dehydration. Regular weighing and checking the volume and colour of the urine should ensure that dehydration doesn't become a problem.

OVERTRAINING

This condition is difficult to spot and may creep up on the cricketer and coach without either being aware of what is happening. It usually occurs when the sportsman or woman increases the training load both in frequency and intensity and then does not allow time enough to eat, sleep, study or work. As performance level drops off the athlete tries to compensate by increasing the training load only to suffer further deterioration in performance falling down the slippery slope and getting involved in a vicious circle of increased work and poor performance. The only sure cure is to rest for four days and increase both the fluid and carbohydrate intake, resisting the temptation to restart training after only one or two days when feeling a little, but not completely, recovered.

WOMEN

Females who have frequent periods may lose enough iron to make themselves anaemic. When anaemia occurs the red blood cells are unable to carry sufficient oxygen to the muscles, resulting in tiredness on and off the field. The doctor can easily correct this deficiency and advice should be sought early. Some women who undergo a lot of endurance training may cease to have any periods, particularly if they reduce their body fat. This condition known as amenorrhoea is quite normal in these circumstances and the periods will return when the training load is decreased. Pregnant women can safely continue to train

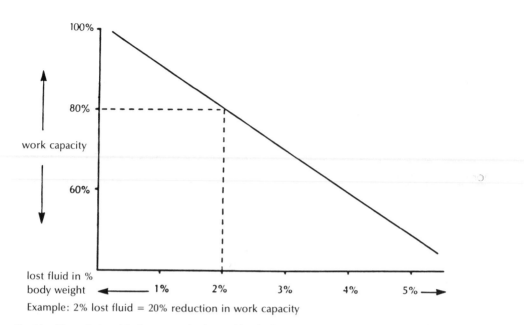

Example: 2% lost fluid = 20% reduction in work capacity

*Fig 61   The relationship between the loss of body fluid and reduction in
work capacity.*

until they start feeling uncomfortable, regular exercise in pregnancy results in healthier babies and easier childbirth for the mother. Playing competitive games is best avoided in order to decrease the risk of miscarriage due to extrinsic injuries.

CHILDREN

Bones continue to grow up to the age of about 18 in males and about 16 in females. However, during growth the bones are not strong enough for the muscles and tendons attached to them, therefore heavy weight training and repetitive high-load training should not be done. As a general rule children should not be lifting more than one third to one half of their own body weight.

In some children the points at which tendons are attached to bones become inflamed, swollen and tender. This may happen just below the knee (Osgood Schlatter's condition) or at the back of the heel (Severs condition).

Boys of 12 to 14 years develop Osgood Schlatter's as do girls between 10 and 12. When they do they may complain of pain just below the knee. They should be allowed to continue to play but should avoid long spells of bowling. The only treatment is to reduce the loading to that particular point, by cutting down on the training until the condition settles. The child can train on resilient surfaces such as grass and during training the use of shock absorbing heel inserts made of sorbothane will prove effective in relieving pain.

Children also develop power and explosive force after puberty and therefore power training should not be undertaken until after this time. Training with very light weights will, however, help with the technical skills of heavier weight training later on.

VETERANS

Older sportsmen and women get no special injuries but as age advances there is more

A near miss. Anticipation and quick thinking can avoid injury when fielding close.

chance of them being injured and the longer it takes them to recover from injury. If you go back to cricket later in life, having had a few years free from sport, start gently with a gradual increase in the frequency and intensity of each session. Secondary injuries may occur in joints previously damaged in earlier years, injuries such as osteoarthritis of the knee joint may develop a long time after a torn cartilage has been removed. These secondary injuries may prevent you from doing as much training as you would like but you will have to adjust to it and perhaps supplement your usual training with swimming and cycling.

TRAVEL

When travelling away from home, whether abroad or in your own country, you may experience difficulty in sleeping especially during the first four nights. A mild sleeping pill may prove helpful at this time and your doctor should be able to help if it becomes a problem. Stay clear of new and untried exotic foods, keep to your usual diet if at all possible and wash any fruit and salads in clean water before eating them. Check that the water supply is safe to drink, if not, stick to bottled water.

When encountering a hot climate the body takes ten days to heat acclimatise. After ten days the salt content of the sweat is reduced and stabilised so that during the first few days all that is required is a little extra salt taken with your food (do not take salt tablets).

If you have a fair skin keep out of the sun, and even if you tan easily avoid sunbathing, otherwise you may become dehydrated. Always wear long sleeves and long trousers at dusk and dawn to avoid unnecessary insect bites and use plenty of insect repellent. Check with your doctor and find out whether any special vaccinations are required well in advance of your trip.

Check-List for Travel

(i)   Vaccinations
(ii)   Food
(iii) Water
(iv)   Heat acclimatisation
(v)   Sleep disturbance
(vi)   Jet lag

DOPING

It is your responsibility as the athlete to ensure that you don't abuse the drug-testing regulations whether intentionally or by error. Mistakes can occur when over-the-counter pain killers, cough mixtures, antidiarrhoea medicines and nasal decongestants are bought which may contain small amounts of codeine and ephedrine. Both drugs are on the banned list and will show up in urine as a positive dope test. Check with the governing body or the Sports Council's Drugs Advisory Group (*see* Useful Addresses) for an up-to-date list of drugs you can and cannot take.

TREATMENT OF SPORTS INJURIES

The aim of treatment is to reduce the amount of damage already done, relieve pain and promote healing. When a sports injury or soft tissue injury occurs, small blood vessels become torn and blood escapes causing bruising and swelling. The action to be taken will help reduce the amount of blood that can escape and cut down on the size of the swelling both of which hinder repair and rehabilitation. Using the mnemonic RICE is an easy way to remember what to do:

RICE   R = Rest
        I = Ice
        C = Compression
        E = Elevation

R = *Rest* is required for the first twenty-four hours following an injury in order to prevent further bleeding.

I = *Ice* is applied to the injury for ten minutes every two hours in the first twenty-four hours. This reduces pain, swelling and further bleeding. The ice should be wrapped in a damp tea towel and must not come into direct contact with the skin (if it does an ice burn may occur). If ice is not available, cold water from the tap will do as will a bag of frozen peas from the freezer.

C = *Compression* of the injury by a firmly-applied crepe bandage prevents further blood escaping and reduces the size of any swelling. The bandage should not be too tight and you may need to re-apply the crepe if it becomes too loose or too tight in the first twenty-four hours.

E = *Elevation* to assist in the drainage of swelling and the prevention of further leakage of blood. The affected limb should be raised above the level of your heart for twenty-four hours.

Treatment of Blisters

The treatment of blisters is dependent on whether or not the skin overlying it is intact. If it is intact the blister is best left well alone. However, if the skin has been broken the blister should be deroofed with a clean pair of scissors. This prevents infection setting in and also assists in the blister bed healing more rapidly although perhaps a little more uncomfortably in the short term. The blister can be covered with a dry, non-absorbent dressing while training, held in place by a piece of tape or strapping.

First Aid

If you are a coach you have a responsibility to know the procedures for basic resuscitation. If and when a serious casualty occurs your first aim is to save life before worrying about the extent of any sports injury. Using the mnemonic ABC helps in an emergency:

A = *Airway*. First, check this and remove any object in the way of air entering the lungs. Remove any false teeth or mouth guards, clear the mouth of vomit or chewing gum and loosen any clothing around the throat. Extend the neck fully in order to prevent the tongue flopping down against the back of the throat.
B = *Breathing*. Second, check that the casualty is breathing – if not, start CPR (cardiopulmonary resuscitation) by giving the kiss of life. Breathe into the mouth of the casualty at the same time as pinching the nose to prevent air escaping from it.
C = *Circulation*. Third, check the circulation by feeling for a pulse. If one is not felt, start compressing the chest wall firmly four times to each breath until the casualty starts breathing and regains a pulse, or until the ambulance arrives.

After the patient has regained consciousness or started breathing by him or herself check for any bleeding. Apply firm pressure with a gauze swab or handkerchief for five minutes in most cases this will be sufficient to stop most major blood vessels bleeding. You can then start assessing the extent of any injury. Try and relieve pain by placing the casualty in a stable position on his or her side and splinting any obvious fractures.

Always check beforehand where the nearest telephone is and send someone to summon the ambulance in order to evacuate the injured person.

First-Aid Box

crepe bandages
gauze squares
zinc oxide tape
elastoplasts
cotton wool
triangular bandage
scissors
antiseptic solution
analgesic (pain-killing tablets)
collar
splints
stretcher
blanket
brooks airway

Rehabilitation

Early rehabilitation of most injuries should be encouraged in order to shorten the time taken to reach a full recovery. In the first twenty-four hours when RICE is applied gentle passive movements are made to assist in the drainage of any swelling and to prevent blood clots forming in the deep veins.

After twenty-four hours more active stretching exercises are performed followed by strengthening exercises. The muscles around an injury rapidly lose power and the co-ordination of muscle movements also worsens within a few hours of the injury being sustained. As the muscles regain power, re-education of skills becomes a priority eventually leading to the ability to get back to training and to playing matches.

Models for Rehabilitation

Grade 1 Injuries

Bruising only has occurred and all that is generally required is the application of RICE in the first twenty-four hours followed by a fairly rapid resumption of normal training.

Grade 2 Injuries — Ligaments/Joints

A sprained ligament on the outside of the ankle joint is a common injury. The principles used in the rehabilitation of this particular injury can equally be applied to the injuries that occur in other parts of the body.

A short-arm pull with the eyes fixed on the ball. Concentration and good technique help to avoid injury during play.

After the first twenty-four hours when RICE is applied you should try to walk on the injured side without a limp in order to stretch any scar tissue that is forming into its correct anatomical alignment; this may mean that you will have to walk very slowly at first. You should then progress to normal walking pace and then start walking and jogging on grass 5m to 10m at a time, increasing to 25m, 50m, 75m and then 100m walk/jog.

When this stage has been reached, continue jogging for up to 400m before starting a few sprints of 5m to 10m followed by sprints of 25m, 50m, 75m and 100m.

At this stage commence running backwards and add weaving and jumping to further strengthen the ankle. Nerves are damaged in a ligament injury and they lose their ability to feed back to the brain the sensation of where in space your foot is in relation to the ground. These nerves have also to be re-educated and this can be done by doing balance exercises. These positional or proprioceptive exercises must be done at the same time as the stretching and strengthening drills. Start by trying to stork-stand on your injured leg and then stork-stand with your eyes closed. After this try throwing a tennis ball up into the air and catching it again while still balancing on one leg, the degree of difficulty can be increased by standing on a balance or wobble board. When you can do all of this regime quite happily for fifteen to twenty minutes you are then fit enough to resume normal training with your squad or team. However, if having done this and your ankle still doesn't feel stable, or if you are unable to play, then advice from a sports clinic or qualified physio-therapist should be sought.

Grade 3 Injuries — Muscles and Tendons

Torn thigh muscles (quadriceps) may occur in fast bowlers landing awkwardly on their front foot. The aim of rehabilitation is to prevent shortening of the muscle or tendon by inappropriate scar tissue formation. Scar tissue may contract for several weeks after an injury. Following the usual RICE application in the first twenty-four hours the quadriceps must be first gently stretched for ten minutes each morning and evening and for a minute every hour during the day. When gentle stretching becomes less uncomfortable more active stretching and static strengthening exercises are undertaken followed by dynamic exercises with increased loadings. Therefore, start with straight leg exercises followed by bending the knee to be followed up by adding weights of between 1kg and 1.5kg attached to the ankle while bending and straightening the knee.

After this the routine of jogging, sprinting, weaving, running backwards together with balance exercises as used for the ankle injury should be followed.

Grade 4 Injuries — Bone Fractures and Dislocated Joints

Most fractures or broken bones, together with joint dislocations, are major injuries and will need a minimum of six weeks immobilisation before any rehabilitation can commence. They require close medical supervision. Stress fractures, however, may only need to be rested for three weeks before gentle progressive training is resumed. If you think you have a stress fracture you should stop training and seek medical advice.

Concussion

If a player is concussed, in other words loses consciousness however briefly with or without memory loss he or she must stop immediately and be examined by a doctor or sent to the nearest casualty department. The player should not be allowed to play again for *three weeks.* If he or she is unfortunate enough to be concussed again the period should be extended to six weeks and if three times in a season he or she should not be permitted to play again for four months.

5 Mental Training

There are now quite a few books on mental training in sport, some of which are listed at the end of this book (*see* the Further Reading section).

However, very few books on specific sports include more than a token section of mental aspects of the sport. This chapter has been written in the belief that a complete training programme must include both the physical and the mental aspects of the game of cricket.

In his book, *The Pursuit of Sporting Excellence* (1986), David Hemery recalls his numerous interviews with a wide range of sport's highest achievers. In response to his question: 'To what extent was the mind involved in playing your sport?' he reported that 'the unanimous verdict was couched in words like "immensely", "totally", "that's the whole game", "you play with your mind", "that's where the body movement comes from" '. Indeed, Clive Lloyd, recalling a great West Indian fightback against the Australians, said that, 'We came out and fought back and brought out the full potential of the West Indies players – mentally and physically.'

In short, we all recognise the importance of having the right mental approach in sport just as we recognise the importance of physical factors. The purpose of this chapter, therefore, is to present a selection of some mental training skills relevant to cricketers (in fact many of the skills are relevant to most people in a wide variety of sports). Before outlining some of these skills, it is important to dispel some of the myths surrounding mental training in sport.

MYTHS AND TRUTHS

Myth 1

'You only need a sports psychologist if you have mental problems.' If that was the case then we would only need to train physically when we were trying to recover from injury! There is no difference between practising physical and mental skills – they should both be practised regularly as a positive aid to performance and not just to offset 'problems' (although they can usefully be employed for this as well).

Myth 2

'All good athletes have a natural mental toughness and don't need to practise mental skills.' Certainly some people will have better mental qualities than others (in exactly the same way that some people are more physically gifted than others). However, that doesn't mean that mental training will not help. Even people like Ian Botham, Imran Kahn and Viv Richards have put in tremendous amounts of physical training even though they are clearly physically gifted people. Natural ability these days is not enough.

Myth 3

'Mental skills cannot be trained or developed.' This is similar to the last myth and it, too, is incorrect. All skills, whether physical or mental can be improved with appropriate practice.

Mental training may not be fully accepted by all people in sport. However, the preceding argument may have convinced you that it is illogical to expect physical training to be the only training in cricket when we all recognise that many games are won and lost on mental factors. Many years ago it was considered slightly odd – even 'unsporting' – to train more than about three days a week. That attitude has long since gone and been replaced with a reluctance to accept regular mental training as a part of contemporary sport. In a few years time, perhaps, we will look back at such an odd attitude with a sense of amusement.

COMPONENTS

In Chapter 3 the various components of physical fitness training were outlined and it was stated then that 'fitness' was best defined in terms of its individual parts. In the same way, it would be naive to say that mental training is just one factor. It is a term given to a number of different components. However, in this book there is not room to cover all of these (interested readers are referred to Further Reading) so we will concentrate on the five basics:

(i)   Relaxation and the control of stress.
(ii) Mental imagery.
(iii) Concentration and mental control.
(iv) Self-confidence.
(v)   Teamwork.

The background to each is explained in brief, including cricket examples. Then, again for each of the basics, some practical mental training exercises are outlined.

However, it should be noted that not all mental skills can be easily taught by coaches without training, although the exercises outlined here have been chosen for simplicity and safety. It is recommended, however, that if mental skills are introduced, they are first done by a registered sports psychologist of the British Association of Sports Sciences (*see*

Useful Addresses). Coaches are also advised to attend courses on sports psychology run by the National Coaching Foundation (*see* Useful Addresses).

Relaxation and the Control of Stress

Relaxation is a much misunderstood concept in mental training as many players think that if relaxation skills are needed, they are needed right before a game. Clearly, being too relaxed is not a good idea, nor is being too tense. The answer, therefore, is to control the 'on/off switch' of the body. On most radios the on/off switch also controls the volume. Seeing that as humans we are 'on' all of the time, the essence of controlling the on/off switch is to control the volume. One way to do this is to learn relaxation skills, of which there are many. Other mental skills, such as mental imagery and concentration, are also dependent upon being able to control the relaxation and activation (arousal) of the body.

In addition to relaxation facilitating rest and recovery in sport, it can have a more immediate effect on performance through reducing anxiety and muscle tension. Moreover, this can relate to self-confidence – another mental skill to be discussed later.

Arousal is the 'intensity aspect' of our behaviour since we often refer to being under-aroused (e.g. drowsy, sleepy) or over-aroused (e.g. over-excited, panicky). In cricket it is easy to get over-aroused with the excitement of the situation. Over-arousal is not necessarily a good thing in sport and can badly affect concentration.

There are many different types of relaxation skills that can be learned, including breathing exercises, muscle tense-relax exercises, and meditation. You will develop your own preference if exposed to the different types and there is no one technique that can be recommended above all others. Two techniques will be outlined here, and others can be found (*see* Further Reading). It should be recognised that not everyone is suited to starting these exercises. For example, people with abnormal blood pressure, a history of cardiorespiratory health problems, asthmatics and those suffering acute anxiety states should all be referred to their doctor beforehand.

Deep Muscle Relaxation

Lie on a mat on the floor with your arms and legs stretched out. Gradually reduce your breathing rate to a slow yet comfortable rate and start saying the word 'Relax' or 'Calm' to yourself as you breathe out. Close your eyes when you feel ready to do so, but do not force it. After about ten exhalations coupled with the word 'Relax', focus your attention on your left leg. Imagine it getting gradually heavier and heavier as you become increasingly more relaxed. Imagine your leg sinking into the mat (concentrating on this for about a minute). Now shift your attention to your right leg and repeat the exercise. This can also be done for your left and right arms in succession. After this you should be quite relaxed and feeling 'heavy' – little or no muscular tension. Slowly sit up, stretch and return to normal activities.

This should be practised for short spells initially as your concentration is likely to be poor. Five minutes may not sound very much but will be plenty for the first session. This form of deep relaxation is best performed several hours before competition to allow you plenty of time for increasing the arousal level to the appropriate point for the game. However, prior to batting, players are advised to calm themselves so that their concentration levels are enhanced.

Progressive Muscle Relaxation

Progressive muscle relaxation (PMR) is a well-known technique for learning the difference between relaxation and tension. It was developed in the 1930s by Edmund Jacobsen and is

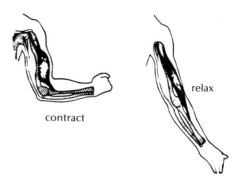

Fig 62   The tense-relax sequence of progressive muscle relaxation.

widely used today in sport, health and other contexts. Essentially, PMR is built on the premise that you will not be able to relax effectively until you can first recognise tension. Consequently, the exercises are a series of tense-relax exercises designed to increase the awareness of muscular tension and relaxation (Fig 62). There is a PMR script which you can either have read to you or which you can yourself record onto tape. It is also possible to purchase relaxation tapes from the National Coaching Foundation (*see* Useful Addresses). Fig 63 shows some of the exercises for PMR.

Relaxation, Anxiety and Stress

We have all experienced the unpleasantness of anxiety in sport; the nervousness before a big game, or the critical point in the match which could swing it either way. However, not all stress is bad. Stress actually refers to any situation when we are 'out of balance', such as when the task appears to be too difficult or too easy for us. The latter will produce the stress of boredom, hence the diagram in Fig 64, which shows that optimum enjoyment is often the result of matching the challenge with the right level of skills; any imbalance could cause stress.

The body prepares for stress through the

117

prayer arm-push

toe-curl (back)

toe-curl (under)

ankle (back)

ankle (under)

knees press

contract thighs

contract buttocks

compress stomach

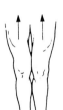

shoulder blades (back)

shoulder blades (forward)

shoulder blades (up)

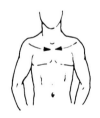

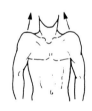

down-reach shoulders

compress chin on to neck

press head on to mat

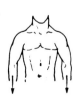

118

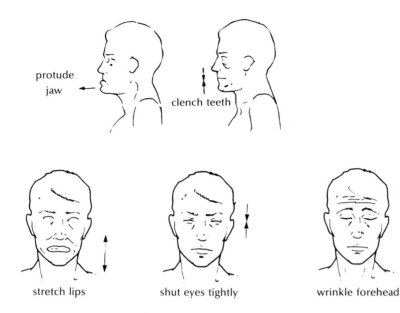

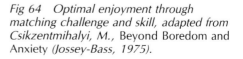

Fig 63 Exercises for tension recognition in PMR.

'fight-flight' reaction, which is the response of the body preparing for action with increased heart rate, breathing rate, adrenalin flow, etc. This feeling could equally be fear or excitement depending on how you see the situation. If you hear footsteps rapidly approaching you from behind in a dark alley late at night you will react with fear if you think it is a mugger. However, if you think it is a jogger you will not react in the same way. In other words, your stress or anxiety response depends on the way in which you see the situation. In cricket you will need to develop relaxation skills and a positive way of looking at the game whenever you become anxious. By practising the relaxation, and other mental skills outlined here, you will be better placed to be able to control anxiety.

Mental Imagery

The ability to visualise events and skills in cricket is another important mental skill which needs practice. It has been known for some time from psychology experiments that men-

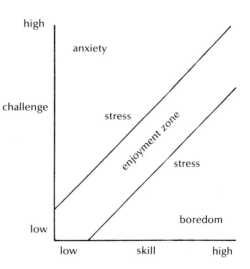

Fig 64 Optimal enjoyment through matching challenge and skill, adapted from Csikzentmihalyi, M., Beyond Boredom and Anxiety (Jossey-Bass, 1975).

TICK ONE

	Yes	In Between	No
(i) Could you 'see' and 'feel' yourself perform the skill?			
(ii) Could you control the picture?			
(iii) Was the picture clear?			
(iv) Was the skill executed successfully?			
(v) Was the skill at normal speed?			
(vi) Did you stay relaxed?			
(vii) Did you stay alert?			
(viii) Did you use senses other than just 'sight' and 'feel'?			

Fig 65   Mental imagery questionnaire. Answer the questions after each of your initial training sessions with mental imagery. This is based on work by Lew Hardy and John Fazey in The Coach at Work *(National Coaching Foundation, 1986).*

tally practising a skill is better than not practising at all, although obviously the best situation is to combine physical with mental practice. But what is mental practice or imagery?

Mental practice is the repetition of a physical skill or movement sequence that is practised through thought and through pictures rather than through actual physical movement. Although the exact reasons why mental imagery works are still not clearly understood, we do know that it does work. Experiments as long ago as the 1930s demonstrated that small electrical impulses could be detected in the muscles from thought alone. This suggests that the 'grooving in' of technique in sport can be accomplished, at least in part, by mental imagery. Such repetitive practice usually works best for predictable skills, such as bowling.

Brent Rushall, a sports psychologist, lists six important guidelines for successful mental rehearsal:

(i)   Your picture should be in the real environment. In other words, if you are wanting to mentally practise a diving catch then 'see' yourself' in a competitive situation – it is more realistic.

(ii)   Perform the skill in full.

(iii)   Make sure the visualisation is successful – avoid rehearsing errors (although this is easier said than done). With practise, though, you should improve the clarity of your mental image and find it easier to control.

(iv)   Visualise the skill before the actual physical performance.

(v)   Imagine the skill at the normal speed.

(vi)   Imagine the skill visually and kinesthetically. In other words, try to feel the movement as if actually performing it. This is best done by visualising yourself actually performing rather than apparently watching yourself on a video.

More useful advice can be found in John Syer and Christopher Connolly's book, *Sporting Body, Sporting Mind*. They suggest that visualisation should follow these guidelines:

(i)   Start with relaxation.
(ii)   Stay alert.
(iii)   Use the present tense.
(iv)   Set realistic and specific goals (*see* later in this chapter).
(v)   Use all of your senses.
(vi)   Visualise at the correct speed.
(vii)   Practise regularly.
(viii) Enjoy it!

Answer the questionnaire (Fig 65) after your initial attempts at mental imagery. This should highlight some of your problem areas for you to work on next time. Remember, keep the initial sessions short and relax beforehand.

Concentration and Mental Control

In Peter Terry's book, *The Winning Mind* (1989), he clearly illustrates the problems of concentration and attention of a player batting in cricket. Often the cricketer has only half a second to recognise, interpret and act on a particular delivery. As Terry writes: 'When a star cricketer like Pakistan's Javed Miandad takes the crease to bat, his concentration processes play a prime role. The virtuoso strokes he produces are only possible through the effective use of several different sensory systems: *vision* to perceive the speed, position and spin of the ball; *hearing* the subtle changes of spin; and a delicate sense of *feel* which permits accurate repositioning of the bat and body in unison.' (This concentration and attention process can be shown in Fig 66.)

We all recognise the importance of concentration but rarely actually practise it as a skill! Try this exercise now but before doing so ensure that you have space around you – i.e. no furniture that you could hit if you fall over!

(Also, it is best to have someone with you just in case you do start to fall over!)

(i)   Stand upright with hands on hips; eyes looking forward. Now take one foot off the ground and rest it against the other shin. How long can you keep your balance without moving the foot that is in contact with the ground?
(ii)   Try the same exercise again, this time with your eyes closed. How long can you keep your balance this time?
(iii)   Finally, try it again, but this time close your eyes and tip your head back. How long can you keep your balance now?

It is probable that your balance got worse as you tried these exercises in turn. But why? These exercises each require concentration to maintain balance, but they become more difficult because they give you less to concentrate on each time.

The first exercise allowed you to have your eyes open, so balance was maintained by concentrating on a combination of seeing and feeling, and that is not very difficult because it is the way we operate in normal life. In the second exercise you were deprived of sight and so only had feeling to help you. If you did not concentrate totally on the small deviations of balance, you probably fell. Finally, in the third variation, the balance mechanisms (in the inner ear) were disturbed by tilting your head back and so – unless you could concentrate superbly on the limited feedback you were getting – you lost your balance easily.

What these exercises illustrate is that, in sport, concentration is the ability to focus on the details around you that are needed for the game and to exclude those not needed. In cricket you need to focus on the ball at the time of delivery rather than on the reaction of the fielders. Many of the top sportspeople interviewed in Hemery's *The Pursuit of Sporting Excellence* rated concentration as a very important factor for them.

Batting demands an instant assessment of the options. Mark Taylor (Australia) decisively scored 1,000 runs in his Test debut year.

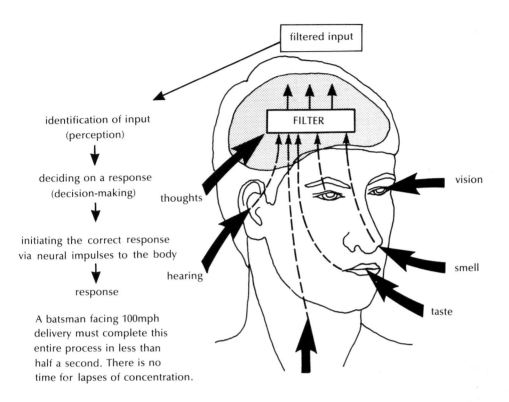

identification of input
(perception)

↓

deciding on a response
(decision-making)

↓

initiating the correct response
via neural impulses to the body

↓

response

A batsman facing 100mph
delivery must complete this
entire process in less than
half a second. There is no
time for lapses of concentration.

thoughts

hearing

filtered input

FILTER

vision

smell

taste

*Fig 66   How sensory input competes for concentration capacity
(reproduced with permission from Terry, P.,* The Winning Mind
(Thorsens, 1989).

A simple exercise to develop concentration is to sit, comfortable and relaxed in a chair and to close your eyes. Then start counting each exhalation starting at one and counting each breath. You need to maintain a state of 'relaxed concentration' to get to the high numbers. Alternately, why not try the balance exercises again? Now that you know what to concentrate on you should be more successful.

Focusing Your Attention

Part of sports concentration, as already suggested, is the ability to attend to the right things at the right time. The process of attention in sport is shown in Fig 66; that attention is made up of at least two parts: direction and focus.

The direction of attention is the internal-external line on the diagram and refers to the extent we attend to things internally (i.e. thoughts and feelings) or externally (i.e. things in our environment).

The other line in Fig 66 is the focus or width of attention (broad-narrow) and refers to whether our attention is narrowly focused (e.g. on the ball) or broadly focused (e.g. on the changing pattern of the field placement). Four main types of attention can therefore be extracted from Fig 66 and applied to different situations in cricket.

The top left square is the broad-internal

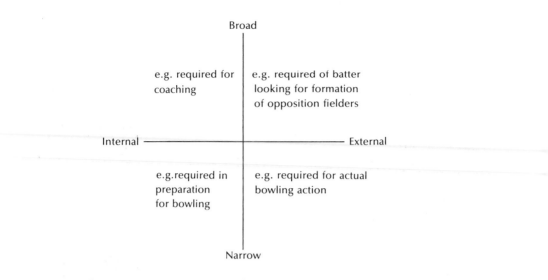

Fig 67   Differing types of attention in cricket.

(analysis) style of attention required by the captain or coach who needs to be able to see things in a broad way – such as the way the entire team is functioning – but at the same time focus internally on thoughts and feelings about the way the game is going, possible changes to be made and so on. The top right square is the broad-external (assessment) focus of attention required by all cricketers. For example, batters not only have to adjust to the way the ball is bowled to them (requiring an external focus), but must also be aware of the positions of fielders (broad focus).

The lower right square refers to the external–narrow (action) focus needed during the execution of a specific skill, such as bowling. This is because the bowler, once committed, should focus on his or her own body movement and skill (narrow) as well as where the ball is to be placed. Finally, the lower left square is internal–narrow and is the focus of attention needed for the preparation of a skill. In cricket this might occur just prior to bowling when attention should be focused narrowly on the exact skill itself.

An American psychologist, Robert Nideffer,

who devised the model in Fig 67, suggests that it is not important just to adopt the right focus of attention at the right time, but it is also critical to be able to *shift* attention from one square to the next as appropriate. Many people in sport are unable to do this effectively because they have a 'preferred style' and tend to stick to it. Clearly, this leads to errors in the game and players and coaches should work on attentional focus and this ability to shift attention.

Self-Confidence

Self-confidence is one of the key areas of mental training for sport. It is very rare indeed for successful sportspeople to have a persistent lack of self-confidence. In understanding self-confidence, four main factors need to be identified. These are: prior performance, demon-

The effectiveness of Ian Botham's medium-paced bowling relies on accuracy and skill in moving the ball through the air and off the wicket.

124

stration and imitation, verbal persuasion and positive self-talk, and monitoring arousal.

The most powerful source of confidence is likely to be your past performances and since success will lead to confidence and confidence to success, a 'positive confidence cycle' can be set up. If your sports performance is improving then all is fine, but what can you do when performance is declining? How can you break into the confidence cycle? One technique which has been shown to be effective is goal-setting (to be considered later in this section). This might include 'going back to basics' to restore successful performance and regain confidence.

The second source of confidence is observation and imitation of others. Coaches can organise highly effective learning situations for cricketers through the use of demonstrations, films and so forth which can act as confidence-building sessions. For example, a player lacking confidence in attacking fast bowling can benefit from watching someone else perform such skills successfully. (However, it is not always such a good idea to show constantly the 'ideal' skill executed by the best player as this may deflate confidence with players saying to themselves 'I'll never be able to do it like that!') Live and recorded demonstrations have been found to be effective, as well as techniques which physically assist players to adopt the correct position. This is more usual in sports such as gymnastics but could be used for some of the skills in cricket (e.g. batting). In addition, players may build confidence through imagining correct skills, so highlighting again the importance of mental imagery.

A third source of confidence is verbal persuasion from others, although it is a relatively weak source of confidence, depending on the people involved; certainly encouragement from a highly respected person can help. A better source of persuasion is likely to come from within the player. Confidence-building statements are sometimes referred to as 'positive self-talk' or 'affirmations'. The most famous one in sport is Mohammed Ali's 'I am the greatest!' Although it may sound odd, there are plenty of examples of people gaining confidence from saying positive things to themselves. (Three techniques for developing posi-

Technique	Method	Comments
'As if' visualisation	Imagine you are someone or something which creates confidence for you. Example: imagine that you have extra large hands when catching.	You can add a positive slogan (*see* below) to go with this exercise.
Positive slogans	Think of a slogan which, when you see it, gives you confidence and direction.	Write it on a card and keep it in a prominent place.
Special words	Think of key or special words which are likely to help confidence, such as 'solid' when batting.	

Fig 68   Techniques for developing confidence through words and images (based on Syer and Connolly's Sporting Body, Sporting Mind).

tive self-talk and affirmations are given in Fig 68.)

A further source of self-confidence can be found in the physiological arousal of the body. If the 'stress response' (referred to earlier) is thought to indicate negative feelings such as fear, then arousal will reduce confidence. A typical reaction here would be for the player, at a critical time in the game, to say, 'I can feel my heart pounding. Hell, I'm scared!' Conversely, if the person sees his or her reaction differently, it could become a positive influence. For example, the player could say, 'I can feel my heart pounding. That's great! I'm ready for this bowler!' Changing such negative thoughts into positive ones can be a useful confidence strategy.

Goal-Setting

One of the best ways to develop confidence and build sound psychological principles into your training is to use goal-setting. Although many people in sport use some kind of planning which approximates to the setting of goals, probably little thought has gone into the best ways of utilising goal-setting. Before outlining a simple goal-setting exercise for cricketers, the following guidelines should be noted:

(i)   Goals can be set for the short-term, medium-term or long-term. To help immediate motivation and action, short- term goals are best. However, think of goal-setting as stair climbing. You are aiming to get to the top (long-term goal) but will need to take one step at a time (short-term goal).

(ii)   Goals should be specific and measurable. Just to set the goal of 'improving my fielding' does not give enough direction. Set a goal that is highly specific and can be measured for success. Feedback based on such measurements is crucial for successful goal-setting.

(iii)   Goals should be realistic but challenging. It is easy to set very high goals, but disappointment will set in if they are not reached. On the other hand, very easy goals will not create extra motivation and direction.

(iv)   Goals should be accepted and worthwhile. For goals to be effective they must be accepted by the participant (hence it is best for the player to be involved in the goal-setting process rather than simply the coach), and considered worth the effort involved.

A goal-setting example for a cricketer is shown in Fig 69. Study this and then complete your own using the structure in Fig 70.

Team-Work

The final topic for mental training that will be considered here refers to team-work. There is no magic formula for getting teams to work well together, although some guidelines may help. Further details can be found in Syer and

Long-term goal	Goals for next month	Goals and action for this week
(i) To be the number one bowler in the club. (ii) To be selected for the county team.	(i) To improve run-up speed (set specific time).	(i) Two sprint sessions (ten x 10m with walk-back recovery in specific time).

Fig 69   Examples of goal-setting in cricket.

Long-term goal	Goals for next month	Goals and action for this week
		(i) (ii)
		(i) (ii)
		(i) (ii)

Fig 70   Your goal-setting chart.

Connolly's *Sporting Body, Sporting Mind* as well as in John Syer's book, *Team Spirit* (*see* Further Reading).

Understanding Others

A key to effective team-work is understanding why other people are playing the game – it may come as a surprise that people do not play cricket for the same reasons. Three main types of reasons have been identified in the past:

(i)   To play to win.
(ii) To play well and demonstrate skill.
(iii) To be part of a team.

Clearly, these differences will exist in players in varying degrees and some may be interested in all three. Nevertheless, coaches, team leaders, etc., may find that knowing their colleagues' main reasons for playing could help relationships within the team and between players and coaches. For example, the player wanting to demonstrate skills will be far less tolerant of being twelfth man than the person who is happy just being a team member.

Team Togetherness

It is often assumed that teams that are cohesive will play better. Although there have been exceptions, this is generally true. However, the cohesion of the team is not a simple matter: players have different personalities and will react differently in various situations.

It is best to view group cohesion in two ways. First, the extent to which players view the team as a whole (i.e. cohesion, togetherness, unity, etc.) and secondly, the degree of attraction the individual player has to the group. Both of these can have two 'orientations', or ways of working – task and social.

A task orientation is where the focus is on getting the job done. This would mean that the team is primarily motivated to play well and win, rather than to enjoy each other's company. A social orientation, on the other hand, is geared towards social relationships rather than group performance. One would expect a social orientation to be stronger in more 'casual' cricket teams and a task orientation to be stronger in high-level teams, although there is no reason why most teams should not possess an interest in both orientations to some degree.

Team Meetings

John Syer and Christopher Connolly have identified three types of team meetings that may be useful in developing mental skills for teams:

(i)   Pre-game meetings: these are for the team to 'warm up' in the emotional and psychological sense. They should be short and to the point.

(ii)   Post-game meetings: these are held at the training session after a competitive game to discuss the team's performance and to plan for the future. Group goal-setting can take place here.

(iii)   Team spirit meetings: numerous discussion topics may be aired, although this meeting will probably not take place very often.

One aspect of mental training that should help the team effort is that if every player in the team makes a commitment to mental training, then this in itself should assist the cohesiveness and 'togetherness' of the team.

POSTSCRIPT

Mental training does provide a positive step towards becoming a more complete cricketer. Everyone will be doing it in the years to come, so why not get a head start?

6 Summary and Programme Planning

In this book we have attempted to provide coverage of the major areas of training for cricket. These include:

(i) skill development
(ii) physical fitness
(iii) nutrition
(iv) injury prevention
(v) mental training

It is not easy to fit all of them into a day-to-day training programme of course. However, each of them should form part of the regular ongoing training programme. Nutrition and injury prevention underpin all sessions. So, having acquired your new-found wisdom, you now need some guide-lines for implementing the programme.

ASSESSMENT

A useful way to start is to assess your current level of training and performance. Only then can a proper 'prescription' and planning exercise take place. For example, assessment may

Training component	PERIOD			
	1	2	3	4
Mental training		**	***	***
Aerobic training		***	**	*
Strength		***	**	*
Muscular endurance		***	**	**
Power		*	**	**
Speed		*	**	***
Flexibility		**	**	**
Individual skills		***	***	***
Team skills		*	**	***

Period 1 End of season recovery up to 2 weeks.
Period 2 Preparatory phase I, out of season, (October to January).
Period 3 Preparatory phase II, pre-season, (February to April).
Period 4 Competition phase.

*** very important
** important
* lower priority (maintenance)

Fig 71 Planning your training throughout the year.

Graham Gooch (England) square cuts off the front foot – the perfect answer to a short delivery wide of the off-stump.

show that you are relatively slow off the mark in running between the wickets or the skill of one hand slip catching needs some attention. These would then feature more extensively in the training programme.

On a more general level, the training plan should follow the following structure:

(i)   End of season recovery.
(ii)   Preparation Phase I (out of season).
(iii)   Preparation Phase II (pre-season).
(iv)   Competition phase (the playing season).

The emphasis in each phase is shown in Fig 72. This outlines a basic plan only and it is likely that different players will have to adapt this to meet their own needs. However, it is impossible to play at a 'peak' for every game. Some priority, therefore, must be placed on different matches. This will require more of a build-up to the important matches, with heavier training loads before some of the less important games. This might mean that the training reverts back to period 3 in Fig 71 for a few weeks before period 4 is performed prior to

the desired 'peak'. Do not try and stay with the training schedules of period 4 for too long as staleness or 'burnout' may occur.

It is usual to change the pattern of training throughout the year to get the best results when required. This is called 'periodisation' or 'cycling' the training year by doing different exercises at different times as stated above. The main reasons for using periodisation are:

(i)   To vary the training load.
(ii)   To aid recovery.
(iii)   To achieve peak performance at a desired time (see Fleck and Kraemer, 1987).

This is particularly important for more advanced players who need to peak for specific matches. However, variety in training should also be applied to beginners as well.

A BALANCED PROGRAMME

A balanced training programme is important for all players. The game itself requires skill,

Level	Physical fitness	Skill training	Mental training
Beginner and club player	Foundation principles across all components.	Basic individual techniques; later team skills for the club player.	Relaxation, arousal control and goal-setting.
County and regional player	Basic components plus emphasis on weaknesses and special needs.	Development of advanced skills.	Problem-solving skills.
National and international player	Specialised intensive training.	Maintenance and development of individual skills; advanced group skills.	Self-sufficiency in mental skills; advanced individual techniques.

Fig 72   Training patterns for cricketers at different levels.

fitness, mental skills, and many more qualities. This means that your training must also reflect such diverse needs. How the playing level might affect the training is shown in Fig 72.

CONCLUSION

Hopefully you can help get closer to fulfilling your own goals of personal improvement and enjoyment through a higher standard of cricket by implementing the training ideas from this book.

Glossary

Aerobic 'With oxygen'; used to describe 'steady-state' exercise where the body relies on oxygen as a continuous source of fuel.

Amenorrhoea Absence of normal female monthly cycle or periods.

Amino Acid The constituent parts of protein: eight of these acids cannot be made in the body (these are termed essential) and must form part of our diet. Another twelve can be synthesised in the body.

Anaemia A deficiency of red blood cells, or of their haemoglobin. Most likely to occur in women with heavy periods or otherwise due to insufficient iron replacement.

Anaerobic 'Without oxygen'; used to describe the energy systems of the body which are used in short, high-intensity exercise.

Basal Metabolic Rate (BMR) A term used to describe the absolute amount of energy required to maintain the body function for life. It is a very precise measure made when the subject is awake, at perfect rest, 12 hours after a meal and in a thermoneutral environment.

Body Mass Index (BMI) A convenient way to express the ratio of height to weight and give a simple estimate of abnormal weight for height. BMI is weight (kilograms) divided by the height (metres) squared and should lie in the range 17–25.

Caffeine A drug found in tea, coffee, chocolate and some carbonated beverages. Promotes fatty acid release, affects the cardiovascular system and is a diuretic.

Calorie A very small, precisely defined unit of heat. One thousand calories are equivalent to one kilocalorie or kcal.

Carbohydrates Molecules containing carbon, hydrogen and oxygen. They may be small simple units, often sweet, such as glucose, sucrose or larger units, often tasteless, such as starch. We cannot digest all carbohydrates and some are termed 'unavailable'; these include cellulose (dietary fibre). Carbohydrates provide energy for the body, about 4kcals per gram or 120kcals per ounce.

Cardiorespiratory Exercise Exercise such as running, cycling, swimming, or any exercise utilising large muscle groups for an extended period of time; develops the ability of the blood, heart, lungs and other systems of the body to persist in work.

Cool-Down A period of light exercise and stretching after vigorous activity.

Dehydration Loss of body fluid with inadequate replacement. Liable to result from excessive sweating, diarrhoea or vomiting.

Dietary Deficiency Inadequate intake of an essential nutrient which results in reduced body stores of the nutrient and eventually affects body function. Diagnosis of a deficiency requires biochemical tests.

Dietary Fibre That part of our food which is not digested by our normal digestive juices and therefore remains in the intestine providing bulk. However, dietary fibre is largely digested by organisms in the large bowel and as such can be absorbed to provide energy.

Dislocation A displacement of the bony surfaces at a joint so that the ends of the bone do not meet, or meet incorrectly. Refer immediately to a doctor.

Doping The use of substances which artificially improve an athlete's performance.

Fats Molecules containing carbon, hydrogen and oxygen. The small molecules are called fatty acids and dietary fats are a mixture of different fatty acids often held together by another molecule of glycerol and are then referred to simply as fat. Fats provide energy, 9kcals per gram or 270kcals per ounce.

Glycogen The form in which the mammalian body stores carbohydrate. It is mainly stored in the liver and muscles and constitutes a very mobile but limited store of energy for the body. It can be used without the presence of oxygen, i.e. anaerobically.

Haemoglobin The oxygen-carrying component of red blood cells composed of an iron-based substance.

Isokinetic A form of resistance training where a machine provides resistance which allows for constant limb speed.

Isometric A form of resistance training where no movement takes place.

Isotonic A form of resistance training involving the lifting of free-standing objects, such as barbells.

Joule A very small and precise measure of the amount of work. The energy in food is related to the amount of work it can generate and therefore sometimes the energy value of food is expressed in joules. One thousand joules form one kilojoule or kJ. One kcal is equivalent to 4.2kJ.

Ligaments Strong bands of fibrous tissue which bind bones together at a joint.

Mental Imagery The process of practising a skill in your mind rather than through physical practice.

Minerals Inert substances some of which are essential to the body for its functioning. Calcium, magnesium, sodium, potassium, phosphorus, iron and zinc are some of these essential minerals.

Muscular Endurance The ability to contract a muscle, or group of muscles, continuously over time.

Nutrients Those parts of food which are used by the body to allow functioning of cells. Carbohydrates and fats are 'burned' to provide energy for cells to work – internally in order to make more tissue, for example, and externally to propel the body. Protein, vitamins and minerals are all used by the cells to function normally.

Osteoarthritis The surfaces of bones at a joint are covered in cartilage which may become worn away, particularly in a joint which has been previously damaged. The joint may be painful, swollen and stiff. This condition is osteoarthritis.

Osteoporosis A condition, mainly in women, in which the bones become increasingly thin and brittle – it is caused by reduced sex hormones and possibly low intake of calcium.

Overload System in which training is progressively increased.

Power The combination of strength and speed.

Progressive Muscle Relaxation (PMR) A form of relaxation training which teaches the recognition of tension and relaxation through a series of muscle-tension exercises.

Proprioceptive Neuromuscular Facilitation (PNF) A form of flexibility training which requires the muscle to be contracted before stretching.

Protein That part of food which contains amino acids. It can be used for energy and provides 4kcals per gram or 120kcals per ounce.

Reaction Time The time which elapses between the stimulus and the start of the movement in response to the stimulus.

Skinfold Thickness The layer of body fat which lies directly beneath the skin which can be measured using skinfold callipers. This layer of fat is related to total body fat and it is impossible to estimate total body fat from this method.

Sorbothane A synthetic substance which absorbs energy well and is used as a 'shock-absorber' for inserts into shoes, mainly at the heel.

Sports Anaemia Probably not a true anaemia; the increase in plasma volume brought on by a serious training schedule dilutes the red cells reducing their concentration, the total number of red cells remaining the same.

Sprain An injury to the ligaments around a joint which may produce pain, swelling and discolouration.

Strength The ability of the muscle to exert force.

Stress Fracture A minute crack in a bone due to repeated overloading by an inappropriately rapid increase in training loads.

Tendon White 'cords' which attach muscles to bones. They may become inflamed (tendonitis), partially torn, or completely broken (ruptured tendon).

Tonicity of Fluid The concentration of particles in a solution compared to the concentration of particles in body fluids, especially blood. If the concentration in a solution is greater than blood it is termed hypertonic; if lower in concentration, hypotonic. Water will always travel from a less concentrated solution to a more concentrated solution.

Variable Resistance Training A form of resistance training which varies the loading to accommodate the mechanical efficiency of the body levers so that optimal tension is placed on the muscle throughout the whole range of movement.

Vitamins Molecules which are found in food and are essential to cells for their efficient functioning. Some vitamins are associated and soluble in fat (vitamins A, D, E, K), others are soluble in water (vitamins B and C).

Warm-Up Light, mainly aerobic and flexibility exercises prior to vigorous activity.

Further Reading

Game Skills

Andrew, Keith, *Skills of Cricket* (The Crowood Press, 1984)

Physical and Mental Fitness

Alter, M., *The Science of Stretching* (Human Kinetics, 1988)

Fleck, S. and Kraemer, W., *Designing Resistance Training Programmes* (Human Kinetics, 1987)*

Fox, E., *Sports Physiology* (Saunders College, 1979)

Hazeldine, R., *Fitness for Sport* (The Crowood Press, 1985)*

Hemery, D., *The Pursuit of Sporting Excellence* (Collins Willow, 1986)

Lear, P. J., *Weight Training: Know the Game* (A & C Black, 1988)

National Coaching Foundation, *Physiology and Performance* (1986)

National Coaching Foundation, *The Coach at Work* (1986)

National Strength and Conditioning Association Journal

Nideffer, R.M., *The Athlete's Guide to Mental Training* (Human Kinetics, 1985)

Railo, W., *Willing to Win* (Springfield Books, 1986)

Syer, J. and Connolly, C., *Sporting Body, Sporting Mind* (Cambridge University Press, 1984)*

Terry, P., *The Winning Mind* (Thorsons, 1989)*

Nutrition

DHSS, *Recommended Amounts of Food Energy and Nutrients for Groups of People in the UK* (Report on Health and Social Subjects No. 15, 1979)

Eisenmann, P. and Johnson D., *Coaches' Guide to Nutrition and Weight Control* (Human Kinetics, 1982)

Haskell, W. *et al.*, *Nutrition and Athletic Performance* (Bull Publishing, 1982)

Ministry of Agriculture, Fisheries and Food, *Manual of Nutrition* (HMSO, 1985)

Paul, A. and Southgate, D., *McCance and Widdowson's 'The Composition of Foods'* (HMSO, 1978)

Sports Injuries

Anderson, B., *Stretching* (Pelham, 1980)

Grisogono, V., *Sports Injuries: a Self-Help Guide* (John Murray, 1984)*

National Coaching Foundation, *Safety First for Coaches* (1986)

Read, M. and Wade P., *Sports and Medicine* (Butterworth, 1981)

St John Ambulance, *First Aid Manual* (Dorling Kindersley, 1982)

* particularly recommended

Useful Addresses

British Amateur Weight Lifters' Association, 3 Iffley Turn, Oxford OX4 4DY.

British Association of Sports Sciences, c/o National Coaching Foundation (*see* below)

National Coaching Foundation, 4 College Close, Beckett Park, Leeds LS6 3QH.

National Strength & Conditioning Association, P.O. Box 81410, Lincoln, Nebraska 68501, USA.

Sports Council, 16 Upper Woburn Place, London WC1H 0QP.

St John Ambulance, Supplies Department, Priory House, St John's Gate, Clerkenwell, London EC1M 4DA.

Index